OUR READERS

Some books you read print fancy reviews written by fancy book critics. Borrring! At the BRI, we care more about what our faithful readers have to say.

"The *Bathroom Readers* are the most interesting and coolest things around. Everyone in my family loves them. I even bought my 10 year-old cousin the 13th edition for Christmas. You guys should win an award!!!"

—**Jennifer S.**

"I'm a teacher and I started perking up the kids in the morning with "Fun Facts" (like the running feet at the bottom of each page). It's an awesome way to dabble in math, geography, science, etc. So, thanks for the little boost you give my classroom!"

—**Dee C.W.**

"Waassssuuuupppp! I just wanted to shout out to all the cool dudes and chicas working on the *Bathroom Reader* staff! I became totally addicted to the *BRs* last year, when my mom gave the 13th edition to my dad for Christmas! Let me tell you, my life hasn't been the same since!"

—**Kim B.**

"I just wanted to say thank you very much for your books. I've learned a lot of different things. And it got my son, (who never even reads a comic book) to enjoy

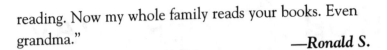

reading. Now my whole family reads your books. Even grandma."

—**Ronald S.**

"You rock! I'm a business and computer teacher, and I've actually used your material in my class. Students can't believe they learn from a book called the *Bathroom Reader*!"

—**Keith B.**

"I am not into reading long, boring books. Ever since I discovered your book, I can't put it down! It's perfect for people like me. Thank you to all the staff at BRI for producing such great reading!"

—**Raelyn H.**

"I'm in 9th grade, and I brought in my entire *Bathroom Reader* collection for show-and-tell at my school, and everybody loved it. Go with the Flow!"

—**Danny D.**

"I've been a reader since the tender age of eight. It first started with shampoo bottles, toothpaste, and deodor-ant directions (yes directions) searching for something else to do aside from the obvious. Bravo to the BRI for making each trip an enjoyable experience."

—**Henrick S-H.**

"My dad gets a new *Bathroom Reader* every Father's Day and I have to wait to read them. When I found out you were making one of your crazy books just for kids, I thought I was going to faint. I love you!"

—**Georgine L.**

Uncle John's
BATHROOM READER
FOR KIDS
ONLY

By the
Bathroom Readers'
Institute

Bathroom Readers' Press
Ashland, Oregon

Dedication:
This book is for all of you who wrote in with discretion
to give us your impressions, ask great questions, and
pass along suggestions. Happy digestion!

THANK YOU!

The Bathroom Readers' Institute sincerely thanks the people whose advice and assistance made this book possible.

Gordon Javna
Jeff Altemus
Jay Newman
Jennifer & Zipper
Julia Papps
Thom Little
Jahnna Beecham
Malcolm Hillgartner
Michael Brunsfeld
Sharilyn Hovind
John Dollison
Bryan Henry
Janet Spencer
Maggie Javna
Sam Javna
Sarah Kaip
Lori Larson
Julia Gunnels
Angela Kern

Allen Orso
Georgene Lidell
Bernadette Bailie
Dylan Drake
Paul Stanley
Rick Rebhun
Raincoast Books
Publishers Group West
Scarab Media
Jess Brallier
Larry Bograd
Marley and Catie Pratt
Illustrated Sandwich
Jeff Cheek
Porter the Wonder Dog
John Javna
Mike Nicita
Mrs. Bragunier
Thomas Crapper

*   *   *

There isn't enough space to list the names of the thousands of kids who have written to the BRI, but without you, this book would have been impossible.

TABLE OF CONTENTS

Because the BRI understands your reading needs, we've
divided the contents by length as well as subject:
Short—A quick read
Medium—2 pages
Long—3 to 5 pages (that's not too long, is it?)

BATHROOM LORE
Short

Medium

LIFE IS STRANGE
Short

Medium

Long

EWW...GROSS
Short

Medium

WILD WORLD OF SPORTS
Short

GREETINGS FROM UNCLE JOHN

Hiya kids,

Welcome to our first-ever *Bathroom Reader for Kids Only*. I send you greetings from the Bathroom Readers' Institute, a little red schoolhouse in Ashland, Oregon, where our dedicated gang of goofy writers created this book. We hope you like it. (And, by the way, you don't *have* to read it in the bathroom!)

For the past fifteen years, we've been making *Uncle John's Bathroom Readers* to entertain adults. But two years ago we asked our readers if they thought a *Bathroom Reader* for kids would be a good idea. Good idea? Sacks of mail and a flood of emails buried us. And that's when we found out how many of our readers were young people. Well, we got the hint and immediately started working on the book you're reading right now.

Here's a little of what you'll find in *Uncle John's Bathroom Reader for Kids Only*:

• Gross stuff. How gross can we get? How about boogers, farts, burps, dandruff, your digestive system (*yuck!*), and my personal favorite: bellybutton lint!

• Weird weather facts—fascinating information on

rain, hail, thunder, lightning, tornadoes, and clouds.

• Stories about amazing kids—like the story about the boy who climbed Mount Everest, the girl who swam the English Channel, and the seven-year-old boy who raised tens of thousands of dollars to help kids in Africa.

• And speaking of amazing kids, check out the amazing story of Sacagawea, the 15-year-old Native American girl who helped Lewis and Clark explore the west.

• A poem I learned in fifth grade, "Jabberwocky." I've loved it ever since and am thrilled to share it with you.

• What else? Elephant jokes, video games, the origins of toys, computer facts, dumb crooks, movie bloopers, sports superstitions, cartoon characters, and a lot more.

I hope you find something new and entertaining in this book—a fact, a story, or a new word—to share with your friends.

So now, from all of us at the Bathroom Readers' Institute, including my trusted assistant, J. Porter Newman, and my talking dog, Elbow Room, remember:

When in doubt…

Go with the Flow!

—Uncle John and the BRI staff

P. S. Check out our website: *www.bathroomreader.com.*

SUPERSTARS

Great sports quotes from some sports greats.

"You miss 100% of the shots you never take."
—**Wayne Gretzky**

"The medals don't mean anything and the glory doesn't last. It's all about your happiness."
—**Jackie Joyner-Kersee**

"It's lack of faith that makes people afraid of meeting challenges, and I believed in myself."
—**Muhammad Ali**

"When I went out tonight I wasn't skating for a gold medal, I was just skating for the pure joy of it."
—**Sarah Hughes,**
Olympic skater

"Excellence is not a singular act, but a habit. You are what you repeatedly do."
—**Shaquille O'Neal**

"You have to expect things of yourself before you can do them."
—**Michael Jordan**

"As long as I can compete, I won't quit."
—**Cal Ripken, Jr.**

"You have to believe in yourself when no one else does—that makes you a winner right there."
—**Venus Williams**

"I can never, ever receive the Most Valuable Player award on behalf of myself. I have got to receive it on behalf of my team."
—**Cynthia Cooper,**
WNBA MVP

"If you can't laugh at yourself, then who can you laugh at?"
—**Tiger Woods**

ODD WORLD RECORDS

Here are some people with way too much time on their hands.

Zolilio Diaz, Spain
Record: Rolled a hoop from Mieres to Madrid, Spain, and back—a distance of more than 600 miles. It took him 18 days.

Travis Johnson, Elsberry, Missouri
Record: Held nine baseballs in his hand "without any adhesives" in 1989.

Randy Ober, Bentonville, Arkansas
Record: Spit a wad of tobacco 47 feet, 7 inches in 1982.

Joe Ponder, Love Valley, North Carolina
Record: Lifted a 606-pound pumpkin 18 inches off the ground with his teeth in 1985.

Steve Urner, Tehachapi, California
Record: Threw a dried, "100% organic" cow chip more than 266 feet on August 4, 1981.

Remy Bricka, Paris, France
Record: In 1988, using 13-foot-long floating "skis," he "walked" across the Atlantic Ocean from Tenerife, Spain, to Trinidad (a distance of 3,502 miles). The trip took 60 days.

The Statue of Liberty's eyes are each 2-1/2 feet wide.

CREEPY CUISINE

People have been eating strange food since…well, since people first felt hungry. How hungry would you have to be to try some of these delicacies?

BATS

That's right, bats. The native people of Guam (an island near Japan) eat them boiled whole. Some bats can weigh up to three pounds, and have wingspans of three feet. It is preferable to leave the fur and the wings on.

SCORPIONS

An Asian delicacy. In Hong Kong, scorpions are pickled in wine, then deep-fried. In other parts of China, they're eaten *alive*, but chefs first get them drunk in alcohol (the hope is that the scorpion will be too drunk to sting).

CRICKETS

In Mexico, crickets are fried, then dusted in chili powder for a delicious crunchy snack (with protein!). They're sold on street corners by the bagful.

TARANTULAS

In Thailand, people eat these big, hairy poisonous spiders roasted and served in coconut cream with lime leaves. Actually, that sounds pretty good (except for the spiders).

One in ten children sleepwalk.

DUMB CROOKS

Here's proof that crime doesn't pay.

PAIN IN THE...

"A Boise man stole a dog at gunpoint, then tucked his gun in the waistline of the back of his pants and drove off with the dog. But the gun began bothering him while he was driving, so he reached back to reposition it and shot himself in the butt. Then, when he tried to remove the gun from his pants he shot himself in the butt again. He was hospitalized in serious condition and the dog was returned to its home."

—Boise Statesman-Journal

THAT WAS UNWARRANTED

"A man who had committed crimes in Morgantown, West Virginia, was curious to know if the police suspected him. He approached two officers and asked if there were any arrest warrants out on him. There were."

—Chicago Sun-Times

BUT WHERE WERE THEIR HELMETS?

"Roger Yost, 40, and William Isberg, 40, were arrested in Fairbanks, Alaska, when they tried to heist a 500-pound safe from a Moose Lodge hall, forgetting that they had arrived at the lodge on bicycles."

—Medford Mail Tribune

Most popular pizza topping in South Korea: tuna fish.

GAMES FROM AROUND THE WORLD

You've probably played hide-and-seek, hopscotch, and kick the can. Here are three games from other countries that you might like to try.

GAME NAME: Dragon
WHERE IT'S FROM: Ukraine
NUMBER OF PLAYERS: 5 to 20

HERE'S HOW YOU PLAY:

1. Choose someone to be the "head of the dragon" and someone else to be the "tail of the dragon."

2. Form a line with the head in front and the tail in back. Put your hands on the shoulders of the player in front of you. Now you are a long dragon.

3. Run!

4. The head of the dragon tries to catch the tail. When it does, it becomes the tail and the game starts again. Play until everyone has been the head of the dragon. The hardest part of this game is keeping the dragon together because you're laughing too hard!

Forget bread: In Japan, kids eat toasted seaweed for breakfast.

GAME NAME: The Moon and Morning Stars
(*La Luna y las Estrellas de la Mañana*)

WHERE IT'S FROM: Spain

WHAT YOU NEED: A large tree

NUMBER OF PLAYERS: 3 or more

HERE'S HOW YOU PLAY:

1. This is a great game for early morning or late afternoon, when the sun is low enough in the sky to cast long shadows—because it's the shadow that will be your playing field.

2. Once you've found the tree, choose one player to be the moon (*la luna*). The moon must stay inside the tree's shadow.

3. All of the other players are the stars (*las estrellas*). They run in and out of the shadow while the moon tries to tag them.

4. If one of the stars is tagged by the moon, that player becomes the moon, and the game begins again.

GAME NAME: Escargot (pronounced *es-car-GO*), meaning "snail"

WHERE IT'S FROM: France

WHAT YOU NEED: A large, flat surface, such as a blacktop, and some chalk

NUMBER OF PLAYERS: 2 or more

Each cell in your body has more molecules than there are stars in the Milky Way galaxy.

DESCRIPTION: This is sort of like hopscotch—with two differences: there is no rock to throw, and the game's shape is not rectangular, but spiral (in the shape of a snail).

HERE'S HOW YOU PLAY:

1. Draw the playing field as shown in the diagram.

2. Using only one foot, hop on all the squares to the center, where you may rest for a moment on both feet.

3. Turn around and hop back on the other foot through the snail to square 1. Then repeat the process.

4. If you make it successfully in and out twice without touching a line or letting your other foot touch the ground, then you get to choose one of the squares to be your "house." Write your name in it. Now you have another square—your house—to rest in. No one else may hop in your house—they have to hop over it.

5) Your turn ends when you step on a line or put both feet down. Then the next person goes.

6) Keep playing until either all of the houses are owned, or it is impossible for any player to make it into the center square. Whoever has the most houses is the winner.

An average of 2,220 Popsicles are eaten in the U.S. every minute.

VIDEO GAME FACTS

In 1951 engineer Ralph Baer had an idea: create a TV you could play games on. Twenty years later, he helped Magnavox release Odyssey—the very first home video game. Here are some facts about the phenomenon he started.

• The first video arcade game was Pong, introduced by Atari in 1972. It was a simple ping pong game: Two lines (paddles) on either side tried to knock a white square (the ball) past each other. It was immensely popular and started the gaming craze.

• *Atari* is an ancient Japanese word. Translation: "You are about to be engulfed."

• In 2001 over 225 million computer and video games were sold—that's about two games for every American household.

• Average age of a gamer: 28 years old.

• Nintendo introduced GameBoy in 1989. Its first game: Tetris (invented by a Russian named Alexey Pazhitnov).

• Biggest release ever: Microsoft's Xbox, released in November 2001, sold more than a million units in its first month.

• Forty-three percent of game players are women.

• In 2000, for the third year in a row, an astonishing 35% of all Americans identified computer and video games as the most fun entertainment activity. Second place: television (18%).

On average, pet guinea pigs live twice as long as pet hamsters.

BODY MUSIC: THE BURP

Your body is a fine musical instrument, making lovely sounds that entertain (and gross out) your friends and family.

STAND CLEAR! ROCKET BLAST!

It's lunchtime. You take a bite of hamburger and a big swig of soda. A few seconds later—*braaaaap!* People at the next table are wondering if the volcano Krakatoa just erupted again or if that noise really came from little old you.

So what exactly was it that made the sound that shook the restaurant windows? Some people call it a burp. Others call it a belch. But whatever you call it, that eruption was 100% gas.

HERE'S HOW IT WORKS

When you eat or drink, you don't just swallow food and liquids. You also swallow air. And air contains two gases—nitrogen and oxygen. These gases need to get out again, so they blast off from your stomach, travel back through your food tube, and out of your mouth.

When you eat or drink too fast, you gulp more air, which gives you more burp power. If you want an even bigger explosion, add some soda pop. Bubbly soft drinks are loaded with carbon dioxide—that's what makes

Why did kings start wearing crowns? One theory: to hide bald spots.

them fizz—and carbon dioxide is another gas. Now you've got carbon dioxide, nitrogen, and oxygen as burp fuel. If you want to add even more firepower, drink that soda through a straw. The straw draws even more air in, which, of course, eventually has to blast back out.

TOO RUDE!

Most people feel that burping in public is impolite. But in some societies, a slight or delicate belch after a meal is considered a compliment. People in Africa, China, Korea, and Japan take it as a sign that you really enjoyed your meal.

X-TREME BURPING

Some kids can burp the entire alphabet (and do it at the dinner table just to bug their parents). Most settle for trying to be the longest or the loudest burper around. The loudest burp on record was made by an Englishman named Paul Hunn. One of Hunn's burps was measured by the *Guinness Book of World Records* at a roaring 118.1 dB (decibels) of loudness. That's louder than a motorcycle (95 dB) and almost as loud as a rock concert (120 dB).

Got a great burp story? Send it to Uncle John.
(*www.bathroomreader.com*)

In Italy, kids smear chocolate "butter" on bread and eat it for breakfast.

COMIC BOOK HEROES

You probably know that Spider-Man got his powers from a radioactive spider bite…but do you know how the character was invented in the first place? Let's take a look at the invention of some classic comic heroes.

SUPERMAN (1938)

The Man of Steel was created as a direct result of writer Jerry Siegel's attempts to meet girls when he was a young man. "I had crushes on several attractive girls, who either didn't know I existed or didn't care," he once explained. "It occurred to me: What if I was real terrific? What if I had something special going for me, like jumping over buildings or throwing cars around? Then maybe they would notice me."

• Siegel and co-writer Joe Shuster named their character after movie actors *Clark* Gable and *Kent* Taylor.

• Superman's hometown was named after the science fiction movie *Metropolis*.

• Lois Lane was inspired by a woman named Lois Amster whom Shuster had a crush on when he was in school.

SPIDER-MAN (1962)

In the early 1960s, Marvel Comics published a comic book called *Amazing Fantasy*. "But after issue number

---

Constipation kills fruit flies more than any other ailment.

ten," publisher Stan Lee recalls, "the sales began to run out of steam...so it was decided that the fifteenth issue would be the final one."

This gave Lee the chance to experiment. "For quite a while," he writes, "I'd been toying with the idea of doing a strip that would break all the rules. A strip that would actually feature a teenager as the star. A strip in which the main character would lose out as often as he'd win—in fact, more often..."

Since Lee had a free hand to do what he wanted in the last issue of *Amazing Fantasy*, he used it to introduce his anti-superhero—Spider-Man.

A few weeks after its publication, sales reports came back. The issue had been a bestseller! That prompted a brand-new monthly comic... *The Amazing Spider-Man*.

BATMAN (1939)

Bob Kane was a fan of the 1926 movie *The Bat*, which featured a villain "who wore an awesome bat-like costume." He also liked to read Sherlock Holmes mysteries. In 1939 he combined the two and came up with Batman.

Twelve comic book episodes later, Kane decided to give Batman a sidekick—one that he conceived as "a fighting young daredevil who scoffs at danger." Both the name and the costume were adaptations of the legendary English hero Robin Hood.

Catwoman was based on the beautiful movie star Jean Harlow, and the Penguin was actually inspired by a character in a cigarette ad.

MOVIE BLOOPERS

Movies may seem well-thought-out, but if you look carefully, you can find all kinds of goofs and flubs. Here are a few we found in recent hit films.

Movie: *A.I. Artificial Intelligence* (2001)
Scene: David (Haley Joel Osmont) jumps into the water in Manhattan and lands in Coney Island.
Blooper: Coney Island is in Brooklyn.

Movie: *Aladdin* (1992)
Scene: As Aladdin and Jasmine sing "A Whole New World," they pass in front of a full moon.
Blooper: When they're near the water, there's a reflection of a crescent moon.

Movie: *Lord of the Rings: Fellowship of the Ring* (2001)
Scene: Frodo and friends are traveling down the river when they pass two giant statues.
Blooper: Both statues have their left arms raised in the air. But after they pass them, a shot from behind shows one statue raising its left arm and the other its right.

Movie: *Bring It On* (2000)
Scene: Torrence's (Kirsten Dunst) little brother, while playing a video game, is making fun of Torrence's

---

488 Rhode Islands could fit inside the state of Alaska.

boyfriend. She gets mad and rips the controller out of his hand.

Blooper: Hello? There's no game in the Playstation, and the disk door is open.

Movie: *Austin Powers: The Spy Who Shagged Me* (1999)
Scene: In the final showdown, Austin (Mike Myers) shoots four bad guys.
Blooper: Listen to the shots—he only fires three times.

Movie: *The Matrix* (1998)
Scene: Neo (Keanu Reeves) is at work.
Blooper: According to the sign on the building, the name of the company is Metacortex. But as he's escaping, there's another sign inside the building, this time calling the company Meta Cortechs.

Movie: *Spider-Man* (2002)
Scene: Spider-Man (Tobey Maguire) gets cut by the Green Goblin (Willem Dafoe) just above his elbow.
Blooper: When the Goblin discovers the same cut on Peter Parker (Spidey's secret identity), it's below his elbow and facing a different direction.

Movie: *Titanic* (1997)
Scene: Jack (Leonardo DiCaprio) is bragging about going ice fishing in Wissota Lake.
Blooper: Wissota Lake is a man-made reservoir built in 1917...five years after the *Titanic* sank in 1912.

UNCLE JOHN'S BRAIN TICKLERS

Ready for a challenge? Have fun with these puzzles.

1. Square Deal. Twenty-four sticks can be arranged to create the pattern below. Can you remove eight sticks from the illustration so that you're left with two squares that don't touch each other?

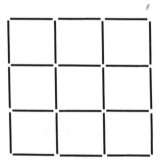

2. Going in Circles. In the drawing below, what number belongs in the center?

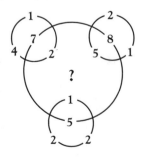

Answers on page 281.

How many baseballs will your favorite pro team use this year? About 18,000.

FAMILIAR PHRASES

Here are the origins to some common phrases.

OVER THE TOP
Meaning: Way too much

Origin: "The expression originated in World War I to describe the method of charging out of the trenches on the attack. Somehow the phrase was later adopted by showbiz people to describe a performance that has gone beyond the bounds of restraint." (From *The Phrase That Launched 1,000 Ships*, by Nigel Rees)

TOP DOG, UNDERDOG
Meaning: Favored, unfavored person

Origin: "Before there were electric saws, all timber had to be cut by hand. Logs were placed over pits specially dug in the ground and two men using a long saw cut the timber. The *top dog* stood above the pit at ground level and guided the saw as it cut. The other man stood in the pit and got covered in sawdust—he came to be known as the *underdog*." (From *Everyday Phrases*, by Neil Ewart)

THAT'S THE TICKET!
Meaning: That's the correct thing

Origin: "This expression of approval has its origin in a mispronunciation of the French word *etiquette*. From 'that's uh-tick'ut,' it was an easy corruption to 'that's the ticket.'" (From *A Hog on Ice*, by Charles Earle Funk)

Galileo called Saturn "the planet with ears."

I WANT MY MTV!

Sure, the world existed before Music Television…
but it was far less interesting.

THE EARLY DAYS

- In 1981 TV exec Robert Pittman had an idea for a new cable station: Get record companies to provide free programming (videos) and have hip VJs introduce them and share "insider" gossip about the stars.

- Sounds like an obvious way to appeal to kids' love of television and music. Yet, when MTV was launched on August 1, 1981, no one imagined it would become so big.

- The first video ever aired was "Video Killed the Radio Star" by the Buggles, which is ironic because that's exactly what happened. The music industry used to be dependent on radio airplay. Today, if you want to make it big in the music business, you have to get your music video on MTV.

GROWING PAINS

- Its first two years were slow. Then, in 1983, New York and Los Angeles began to offer MTV on their cable systems. By 1986 it was seen in 28 million homes.

- Stars like Michael Jackson, Madonna, and U2 saw the potential of MTV and created elaborate videos to showcase their songs. It worked: both MTV and the performers became mega-popular.

There are 32 leather panels and 642 stitches on a regulation soccer ball.

- By the late 1980s, MTV had become…well, boring and predictable. How did they spice up the format? They added shows like *MTV News*, *Yo! MTV Raps*, *Remote Control*, *TRL*, *Beavis and Butt-Head*, and *Unplugged*.

WE ARE THE WORLD

- MTV Europe was launched in 1987, followed by MTV Asia in 1991 and MTV Latino in 1993.

- MTV became a political force during the 1992 presidential election. Its "Rock the Vote" campaign encouraged young people to register to vote. Presidential candidates were invited to discuss issues on the air with first-time voters. Among the candidates taking advantage of "Rock the Vote" was Bill Clinton, whose appeal to young people helped him get elected.

- Twenty years after MTV aired the first video, they introduced a new show, featuring the daily life of aging rock star Ozzy Osbourne and his family. *The Osbournes* quickly became the most-watched show in MTV's history.

- Today, it's estimated that a billion people in 164 countries watch MTV in 18 different languages.

MTV FACTS

- Michael Jackson was the first black artist to have a video aired on the music channel.

- In 1992 MTV started the reality TV craze with *The Real World*.

- Got their start on MTV: Pauly Shore, Carson Daly, Jon Stewart, Carmen Electra.

Population report: New Zealand has about four million people…and 70 million sheep.

A WORLD OF SCHOOL LUNCHES

Ever wonder what kids are eating at school in other countries?

JAPAN. Most schools don't have cafeterias, so kids eat in their classrooms. Schools serve a variety of meats, fishes, vegetables, and sea plants. A typical meal consists of stew (or curry), boiled vegetables, a sandwich, and salad, with milk and ice cream.

MEXICO. The school day ends at 2 p.m., so kids usually wait until they get home to eat. But for kids who are really hungry, vendors wait outside with spicy snacks: watermelon and hot sauce, cucumber spears doused in chili powder, and popcorn with salsa.

FRANCE. By law, kids are not allowed to bring a lunch to school. But they do get a two-hour break to eat a gourmet meal in the *cafétéria* ("cafeteria"). Sample lunch: They start with a beet and endive salad, followed by hen with rice in white sauce, Camembert cheese, and for dessert, chocolate mousse.

GERMANY. Most schools don't have kitchens, so they have the meals delivered. Students eat in the *Speisesaal* ("dining room"). A typical lunch consists of chicken schnitzel (a breaded cutlet) with sauce, mixed vegetables, and salted boiled potatoes.

Beethoven published his first composition when he was only 12 years-old.

STUPID PET TRICKS

They're not stupid, and they're not tricks. But they are funny.

LICENSED...TO DRIVE?

In Germany, an angry driver jumped out of his car to confront the driver that had just smashed into him. Surprise! The person sitting behind the wheel was...a dog. Police say the dog had jumped into the front seat and accidentally released the hand brake.

FIGHTING LIKE CATS AND DOGS

Police in Montana responded to an emergency call on Christmas Day. When the officers arrived, no one was home but they noticed that the family's pets were fighting. What had happened? The angry pets had knocked over the phone and the speed dial had automatically called 911. The mischievous animals were not taken into custody. After all, it was Christmas.

VIP (VERY IMPORTANT POULTRY)

Looking for a place to stay in Memphis, Tennessee? Try the Peabody Hotel—it's loved by celebrities, dignitaries and...ducks. Every day at 11 a.m., the Peabody Marching Ducks take an elevator to the lobby and parade down a red carpet to the sounds of a John Philip Sousa march. Destination: The lobby fountain, where they spend the day. At 5 p.m. when the music strikes up again, they march back to the elevators and up to their home on the roof. This has been a hotel tradition for over 30 years!

Glass never wears out—it can be recycled forever.

HERE COMES THE SUN

Some facts about that big lightbulb in the sky, from astronomer (and BRI member) Richard Moeschl.

• It takes 8.3 minutes for the sun's light—traveling at 186,282 miles per second—to reach Earth.

• The sun looks yellow-gold because we're viewing it through Earth's atmosphere. Judging from its surface temperature, the sun's color is probably closer to white.

• The temperature of the sun at its core is around 73 million degrees F.

• English astronomer James Jeans once figured that if you placed a piece of the sun's core the size of the head of a pin on Earth, its heat would kill a person 94 miles away.

• The temperature of the sun's *photosphere*, the part that sends us light, is about 10,000 degrees F.

• The sun produces more energy in one second than human beings have produced in all of our history. In less than a week, the sun sends out more energy than we could make by burning all the natural gas, oil, coal, and wood on Earth.

• The amount of power that falls on each square foot of Earth's surface per minute is about 126 watts, enough to light two standard 60-watt lightbulbs.

• With every passing day, the sun loses energy, but don't worry—it still has about 5 billion years of life left in it.

THE KID WHO PEED OUT THE FIRE

We'd like to nominate this amazing kid for an award to honor his uncanny ability to think on his feet. Here are some fireworks you've (probably) never seen.

I t all began in Philadelphia on July 4, 1777, when people started to celebrate by shooting rifles, lighting candles, waving banners... and Independence Day was born.

But no 4th of July can match the celebration of 1854 in Bristol, Rhode Island. That year, several houses were accidentally set on fire by firecrackers and by the wadding (a small piece of cloth used to pack the gunpowder) from fired guns. But a kid saved the day. Here's the actual account from the local newspaper, *The Bristol Phoenix,*

"A portion of the wadding of one of the guns lodged upon the roof of the Baptist church and set it on fire.... A lad named Morris, about twelve years of age ascended by the lightning rod and attempted to extinguish the flames by scraping dust upon them with his feet, but finding it of no avail, he began to spit upon them, still flames increased until he had the presence of mind to unbutton his pants and play his own engine so effectually that he entirely extinguished the fire."

According to the *Phoenix*, a large crowd saluted the lad with loud "huzzahs." That's the spirit!

VIDEO TREASURES

Ever found yourself at a video store wondering which ones are worth watching? It happens to us all the time—so we decided to offer a few recommendations.

CLOAK AND DAGGER (1984) *Suspense*
"A highly imaginative boy who often plays pretend spy games with his fantasy friend, Jack Flack, and finds himself involved in a real life-and-death situation. Suspenseful and fast-paced, but not scary or violent." (*Video Movie Guide*)

5,000 FINGERS OF DR. T. (1953) *Fantasy*
"Largely ignored, one of Hollywood's best fantasies, devised by Dr. Seuss. A boy has a nightmare about a cruel piano teacher ruling over a land where kidnapped youngsters are forced to practice the piano." (*Leonard Maltin's Movie and Video Guide*)

SOUNDER (1972) *Drama*
"During the Great Depression, black sharecroppers in the deep South endure various hardships. Well-made family movie." (*Halliwell's Film and Video Guide*)

HARRY AND THE HENDERSONS (1987) *Comedy*
"Ordinary American family vacationing in the Northwest has a collision with Bigfoot. Thinking that the big guy is dead, they throw him on top of the car and head

home. Nice tale efficiently told, with John Lithgow as the frustrated dad trying to hold his Bigfoot-invaded home together." (*VideoHound's Golden Movie Retriever*)

THE LAST UNICORN (1982) *Fantasy*

"Well-written and nicely animated feature about a magical unicorn who goes on a quest to find the rest of her kind. Strong characters and a lively pace make this one a gem." (*Video Movie Guide*)

THE SECRET GARDEN (1993) *Drama*

"A young, lonely, orphaned girl, sent to live with her wealthy uncle, helps her sick cousin back to life. A charming, deftly made version of the classic children's story." (*Halliwell's Film and Video Guide*)

THE GOONIES (1985) *Adventure*

"A bunch of kids go in search of hidden treasure in this old-fashioned adventure tale. Big, lively, and exceptionally noisy, with a likable bunch of kids onscreen." (*Leonard Maltin's Movie and Video Guide*)

THE PRINCESS BRIDE (1987) *Fantasy*

"A modern update of the basic fairy tale, this adventure story centers around a beautiful maiden and a swashbuckling young man as they battle the evils of the mythical kingdom of Florin to be reunited with one another. Fun for adults as well as children." (*VideoHound's Golden Movie Retriever*)

BASEBALL SUPERSTITIONS

When a major-league baseball player is in a slump, he usually spends some extra time practicing. For some, though, that's not enough. Here are a few of the superstitions players follow for luck.

• **Wade Boggs**, one of the game's all-time best hitters, ate chicken before every game.

• Dodger manager **Tommy Lasorda** always ate linguine before a game—with red clam sauce if the team was facing a right-handed pitcher, white clam sauce if it was a lefty.

• Pitcher **Luis Tiant** wore a special loincloth around his waist under his uniform to "ward off evil."

• During **Leo Durocher**'s 40-year career as a player and manager, he'd keep winning streaks alive by not changing his clothes—underwear included—until his team lost.

• **Babe Ruth** *always* touched second base on his way to the dugout at the end of each inning. **Willie Mays** always *kicked* second base as he left the field.

• Red Sox shortstop **Nomar Garciaparra** steps on each dugout step with both feet when he enters the field.

• Yankees shortstop **Phil Rizzuto** put a wad of gum on the button of his cap and only removed it when the team lost.

AESOP: FACT OR FABLE?

A fable is a short story with a moral or lesson at the end. People have been telling them for thousands of years. And the whole tradition started with a man named Aesop.

BACKGROUND

If you were asked to name the most influential writers in Western history, you might include Shakespeare, Hemingway…or even Dr. Seuss. But you probably wouldn't think of Aesop.

Yet his stories have been around for more than 2,000 years, and he's had an impact on everything from ancient Greek philosophy to modern American culture. Expressions like "don't cry over spilt milk" and "sour grapes," for example, come from his fables.

On the other hand, Aesop wasn't technically a writer. Nothing was written down during his lifetime; oral tradition kept his legend and his fables alive. So, the question is: Did he really exist?

Scholars are fairly certain that he did—and that he was much admired as a storyteller. "The best evidence of Aesop's life comes from remarks about him in ancient sources like Aristotle and Plato," writes Leo Groarke of Wilfrid Laurier University in Ontario, Canada.

A BRIEF BIOGRAPHY

Scholars have established a few facts about Aesop's life:

• He was born a Greek slave in the sixth century B.C.

• He had a natural gift for creating fables and became famous in ancient Greece because of it. Eventually his skill for storytelling earned him his freedom.

• As a free man, Aesop traveled widely until Croesus, the powerful king of ancient Lydia, invited him to become an ambassador. He was sent to various parts of Greece, trying to establish peace "by telling his wise fables."

• Aesop's last diplomatic mission was to Delphi where Croesus gave him gold to hand out to the citizens. But Aesop was so offended by the people's greed, he sent the loot back to Croesus. The Delphians became so enraged that they accused Aesop of being irreverent and disrespectful—a major crime—and executed him. According to legend, they pushed him off a cliff.

• Following his execution, a myth grew around the incident. It was said that a series of calamities befell the citizens of Delphi. The disasters got worse until, finally, the people publicly confessed their crime. After that, "the blood of Aesop" was a common reference to the fact that evil deeds will not go unpunished.

People used to believe that seeing a dog eating grass meant a rainstorm was coming.

HOW THE FABLES WERE SPREAD

After his death, Aesop became a sort of mythical figure (like Mother Goose). Fables were automatically credited to him, no matter who invented them. And he remained famous for a thousand years after his death. But with the coming of the Dark Ages, he was mostly forgotten.

FABULOUS COMEBACK

Then, in the 1300s, a Turkish monk named Planudes assembled a collection of Aesop's fables. When Italian scholars of the 1400s became interested in ancient history, Planudes' book was one of the first works they translated and printed, along with works by Homer and Aristotle.

Aesop's tales spread from Italy to Germany, where the religious leader Martin Luther translated 20 of the fables and said that next to the Bible, he valued *Aesop's Fables* above all other books.

A MAJOR WORK

Finally, in 1610, a Swiss scholar named Isaac Nicholas Nevelet printed a version of Aesop's fables called *Mythologica Aesopica*. It was popular throughout Europe and made Aesop a permanent part of Western civilization.

"No book," wrote the editor of a 19th-century collection, "with the exception of the Bible, has had a wider circulation than *Aesop's Fables*. They will be read for generations by the inhabitants of all countries."

Fancy name for a person who collects teddy bears: an *arctophile*.

TODAY'S FORECAST: RAIN... WITH A CHANCE OF FROGS

Throughout history, people have reported all kinds of things dropping out of the sky. Here are a few real-life examples (not cats and dogs—but fish, frogs, and other surprises).

• In May 1981, thousands of green frogs weighing only a few ounces each rained down on the city of Naphlion, Greece.

• On June 6, 1869, residents of Chester, Pennsylvania, were treated to a light rainshower filled with snails.

• On January 15, 1877, live snakes fell on Memphis, Tennessee.

• On June 27, 1901, a heavy rain at Tiller's Ferry, South Carolina, dropped hundreds of small catfish, perch, and trout on people's heads.

• A substance that many people describe as "angel hair" has dropped from the sky on numerous occasions. Scientists think this silky material could actually be thousands of spiderwebs.

• In Chico, California, oval-shaped rocks began to fall out of the sky in July 1921 and continued to fall off and on for *five months*!

Frogs can get athlete's foot.

THE NAKED TRUTH

Some people find nudity shocking. To Uncle John, stupidity is far more shocking. These characters demonstrate that whether you're dressed or naked, you can still be dumb.

On Strike? "A Wisconsin bowling alley decided to jazz up the sport with a little humor. They posted signs reading BOWL NAKED, BOWL FREE. No one took them up on the offer…until April 16, 1996. That's the day 21-year-old Scott Hughes rented a pair of shoes and proceeded to take off his clothes. As a local church group watched in horror, he went on to bowl a 225 game—wearing nothing but a cowboy hat and bowling shoes." (*Knuckleheads in the News*)

Sound Fishy? Francesca Nortyega, a well-known European reformer, willed her estate to a niece on the condition that she keep the family goldfish outfitted in pants.

Washed Up? In 1995 San Francisco mayor Frank Jordan, running for re-election, tried to show he was a "regular guy" by accepting a challenge from two disc jockeys to take a nude shower with them. Photos of the shower circulated all over the city. He lost the election.

Too Cool? "Madame de la Bresse directed that her life savings of 125,000 francs be used to buy clothing for naked Paris snowmen. In 1876 the courts upheld the will, making French snowmen the best dressed in the world." (*Best, Worst, & Most Unusual*)

THE PONY EXPRESS

Here's a classic Hollywood scene: A town in the Old West.
Everyone's waiting for the Pony Express to arrive with the mail.
Well, it turns out that it didn't exactly happen that way.

T**HE MYTH**
• Most people believe that the Pony Express was one of the most important links connecting the Gold Rush towns of the West with the large Eastern cities—but that's a myth. It was actually a flop.

• Before the Pony Express, a letter going from New York to California first went by boat from New York to Panama, then 50 miles across the isthmus of Panama by mule or by train, and then by boat (again) from Panama to San Francisco. A letter was rarely delivered in less than a month.

• In its short lifetime (18 months—between 1860 and 1861), the Pony Express *was* the fastest way to send a letter to California. Riders could deliver a letter in only 10 days. But the Express had major problems.

WHY IT WAS A FLOP

• Hardly anyone could afford to use it. At first, a single letter cost $5 to mail (the price did go down, but never dropped below $1). The biggest customers were newspapers that depended on late-breaking news to keep readers up to date.

• The shipping firm of Russell, Majors & Waddell—

founders of the Pony Express—knew their enterprise could never make money with regular business. They were counting on winning a contract with the federal government to help pay their enormous expenses. But the government was more interested in another promising innovation—Samuel Morse's telegraph.

• By 1861 the nation's first transcontinental telegraph line was completed—making the Pony Express obsolete overnight.

PONY EXPRESS FACTS

• There wasn't a single pony in the Pony Express. Ponies couldn't carry large loads of mail over long distances. Full-sized horses were used.

• Few of the riders were adults (they weighed too much). Most were teenagers hired through newspaper advertisements. Here's a typical ad for a Pony Express rider:

> Wanted: Young, skinny, wiry fellows, not over 18. Must be expert riders willing to risk death daily. Orphans preferred.

By the time you reach age 72, you'll have eaten about 35 tons of food.

ASK THE EXPERTS

*Everyone's got a question or two they'd like
answered. Here are a few questions, with
answers from some top trivia experts.*

STUCK ON YOU

Q: *Why do tongues stick to cold metal?*

A: "It's not only our tongue—it's any warm, wet body part. 'It becomes "flash frozen" to the cold object,' notes geochemist John Kelley of the University of Alaska. 'Because metal is such a good conductor, the heat of your body is immediately transferred, and all surface moisture becomes crystallized.' The classic treatment is to pour warm water on the compromised appendage. This will melt the ice crystals, but will do little to restore your sense of pride." (From *Why Moths Hate Thomas Edison*, edited by Hampton Sides)

DOES ZIT REALLY MATTER?

Q: *Will I really get zits if I eat chocolate, fried foods, etc?*

A: "No. The good news from the dermatologists is that that's just an old wives' tale. In a study performed at Yale University, teens consumed large amounts of chocolate. Even those who were prone to acne didn't show a significant difference. In fact, doctors say that there are no foods that cause pimples—unless you're allergic to a specific food, in which case the allergy shows up as a rash. Since adults can eat chocolate and fried foods without breaking out, this is obvious common sense." (From *Old Wives' Tales*, by Sue Castle)

THE ROOT OF THE PROBLEM

Q: *Why is root beer called "beer" when it isn't beer at all?*

A: "It's pretty much consumer fraud. In the early 1870s, Charles Hires was served a root and herb tea at a country inn, and liked it so much he decided to market it as a soft drink. As an anti-alcohol prohibitionist, Hires hoped that drinkers would abandon liquor in favor of his root tea. But just to be safe, he decided to call it a 'Root Beer.'

"The ploy worked well. In fact, too well. The success of root 'beer' brought down the wrath of the Women's Christian Temperance Union, which called for a boycott of the soft drink. From 1895 to 1898, a war against root beer was waged in the newspapers, nearly destroying the Hires Co. Finally, an independent lab analyzed samples of the soft drink and concluded that root beer contained 'less alcohol than a loaf of bread.' The WCTU apologized, and sales of Hires Root Beer rebounded." (From *Just Curious Jeeves*, by Jack Mingo and Erin Barrett)

*　　*　　*

REAL-LIFE SIGNS IN ENGLISH
FOUND IN FOREIGN COUNTRIES

On a Viennese restaurant menu: "Fried milk, children sandwiches, roast cattle and boiled sheep."

In a Swiss inn: "Special today—no ice cream."

The Native Americans of New Mexico have been eating popcorn for more than 5,000 years.

HOW WE GOT THE DOLLAR

Ever wonder why we call our money "dollars"?
Well, we've got the answer for you.

BACKGROUND

In 1519 Stephan Schlick, a Czech nobleman, discovered a rich vein of silver on his estate in the Joachimsthal Valley. He began minting his own coins, which were accepted as equal to *groschen*—the official currency of the Holy Roman Empire—in 1520.

Schlick's coins were first referred to as *Joachimsthaler-groschen*, after the valley in which they originated. But that was too hard to pronounce, so people began shortening the word. The coins became known as *thaler-groschen*, and eventually just *thalers* or *talers*.

What Goes Around...

Schlick and his neighbors produced millions of thalers. By 1600 there were 12 million of the coins (an enormous amount for the time) circulating around Europe. One result was that the value of the thaler changed from region to region.

After a while, the term *thaler* didn't even refer to Schlick's money anymore. It became generic, referring to any large silver coin. Eventually, different cultures came up with their own version of the word. In Italy,

---

Your fingernails grow four times as fast as your toenails.

for example, a large silver coin became known as a *tallero*; in Holland, it was a *daalder*; Sweden had *dalers*; in Hawaii, silver coins were *dalas*; Ethiopians exchanged *talari*, and in English-speaking countries, a silver coin was called a *dollar*.

COMING TO AMERICA

The term *dollar* was particularly popular in Scotland. As Jack Weatherford writes in *The History of Money*:

> The Scots used the name "dollar" to distinguish their currency, and thereby their country, more clearly from their domineering English neighbors to the south [who used *pounds*, *shillings*, *pence*, etc.]. Thus from very early usage, the word "dollar" carried with it an anti-English or anti-authoritarian bias that many Scottish settlers took with them to their new homes in the Americas.

THE AMERICAN WAY

That explains how the term *dollar* got here...but not why it became the official currency of the United States. After all, American colonists were mostly still loyal British subjects and would have preferred English currency.

The problem was that the colonists suffered from a constant shortage of all coins—especially English ones. Starting in 1695, laws to keep gold and silver inside Britain's borders were passed by Parliament. "Britain forbade exporting gold and silver to anywhere in the world," Weatherford writes, "including its colonies."

For a while, the colonies minted their own money. But

in the mid-1700s, Parliament prohibited that, too. As a result, the only coins available to American colonists in adequate supplies were Spanish silver *reales* (pronounced ray-ahl-ehs; "royals" in Spanish), which were minted in Mexico, Bolivia, and Peru. The colonists did not call them *reales*, though; they preferred the already familiar term *dollar*.

By the time the colonists declared independence from Britain in 1776, the "Spanish dollar" was the accepted currency of the United States.

WHAT NOW?

In 1782 the new nation began to address the issue of a national currency. Thomas Jefferson pointed out that the dollar "is the most familiar to the minds of the people. It is already adopted from south to north."

So on July 6, 1785, Congress declared that "the money unit of the United States of America be the dollar." Interesting note: Neither Jefferson nor Alexander Hamilton, the first secretary of the treasury, liked the term. Though they wrote laws that used the term "dollar," they did it, Weatherford says, "with the idea that they would think of a better name later."

The new government allowed the Spanish dollar to continue as unofficial U.S. currency until the U.S. Mint was finally in operation nine years later. The dollars it first turned out were silver coins—not paper like we use today. It wasn't until many years later that the dollar bill came into existence.

Can you find them all? There are 293 different ways to make change for a dollar.

GROSS BODY FACTS

Bored? Impossible! After all, that body you're living in is like a never-ending carnival of the bizarre, gross, and unbelievable. Seriously! Check out how busy you are!

- You shed dead skin cells at a rate of about 40 pounds per lifetime.

- Eating asparagus can make your pee smell funny. Eating red beets can turn your pee red. Do both at once, and wow, talk about fun!

- Your feet can sweat as much as a gallon of perspiration per week.

- One advantage to blowing your nose when it's full: what comes out is full of trapped dirt and unwanted germs.

- Every day you burp about 15 times, swallow a quart of snot, and make eight cups of pee. (If you eat fast and talk while you chew, you'll burp even more.)

- You make a quart of saliva every day and a new batch of snot every 20 minutes.

- Ear wax captures dirt that shouldn't get to your inner ear. How do you get rid of it? Opening and closing your mouth—that breaks the wax into teeny pieces, which then fall out.

- About 75% of the dust floating around your house is dead skin cells.

- Your body's odor is caused by bacteria that live in your sweat—multiplying, dying, and decomposing.

- Don't try to stop yourself from throwing up by closing your mouth—it'll come out your nose.

It takes a chicken 24 to 26 hours to make an egg.

OOPS!

Everyone enjoys reading about someone else's blunders.
So go ahead and feel superior for a few minutes.

GOTTA GO

"In Morro Bay, California, a prisoner on a highway work detail was using a Porta Potti when a truck driver, unaware the toilet was occupied, hooked it up to his truck and began towing it down the freeway to another site. The prisoner was rescued when the drivers of other cars on the freeway called 911 to report they'd seen him standing inside the Porta Potti with the door open yelling, 'Hey! Help!' as the truck sped down the highway."

—**"The Edge," The Oregonian**

YOU'RE FIRED

"Firefighters in Kushima, Miyazaki, Japan, accidentally set their fire truck on fire while responding to an alarm. Apparently, they left burning cigarettes in the cab of the truck."

—**Bonehead of the Day**

THE LIGHTS ARE ON, BUT...

"Police in Oakland, Ca., spent two hours attempting to subdue a gunman who'd barricaded himself inside his home. After firing 10 tear gas canisters, officers discovered that the man was actually standing right beside them, shouting pleas to come out and give himself up."

—**Bizarre News**

ANIMAL MAGNETISM

Attention Disney: Looking for an idea? Here are a few real-life stories of unusual animal friendships.

FISH + DOG

Chino is a nine-year-old Golden Retriever with fuzzy paws. Falstaff is a freshwater fish who likes to nibble on fuzzy paws. The two have been friends for three years, according to Mary and Dan Heath of Medford, Oregon. They say that as soon as Chino discovered the fishpond in the backyard of their new house, he began lying on the rocks, watching the fish. Chino's favorite fish is Falstaff, a 15-inch orange-and-black koi. And the feeling is mutual. When Chino lies down with his nose an inch from the water, Falstaff swims up to the surface and playfully nibbles on the pooch's paws.

MOOSE + COW

When a moose wandered out of the Vermont woods and fell in love with a Hereford cow named Jessica, it made headlines around the world. For 79 days, the moose stayed by Jessica's side, nuzzling her with his big velvety snout and often resting his head on her back. So many people liked this love story that Pat Wakefield wrote a book about it, called *A Moose for Jessica*.

The signals your brain sends to the rest of your body travel at about 200 mph.

DOG + DUCKS

When seven-year-old Louise Hammond heard little squeaks coming from an underground pipe at the Brooke Marine boatyard in Aberfoyle, Scotland, she immediately told her father. Her dad crawled through the two-foot pipe and rescued a group of baby mallards. As each duckling was pulled from the pipe, Ben, the family dog, gently licked them clean. It was love at first sight. Ben, a German Shepherd, became their ducky dad. And they became his puppy pals. Now the ducklings follow Ben everywhere. They are with him inside the house and out and they even swim together in the backyard pool.

GORILLA + KITTEN

Koko is a remarkable gorilla who lives at the Gorilla Foundation in Woodside, California. What makes her so amazing is that she speaks sign language. Koko can understand over 1,000 words.

In 1984 Koko asked Dr. Penny Patterson, her trainer, for a cat. So when some abandoned kittens were brought to the compound where Koko lives, she was given the pick of the litter. After examining the kittens carefully, Koko chose a little gray kitten that she named All Ball. Koko was very gentle with the kitten and treated him like a baby gorilla, carrying him on her back. When All Ball was hit by a car, Koko cried for two days. (But life goes on... Koko has since had several other kittens, including Lipstick and Smoky.)

The first public zoo in the United States opened in Philadelphia in 1874.

CAT + BIRDS

You'd think that three baby song thrushes, having fallen out of their nest and lying helplessly on the ground, would be in serious danger when a cat is near. But not in this case.

Jerry the kitty was lounging around in his Gloucestershire, England, yard when he noticed the three young birds. Abandoning his feline instincts, he didn't attack...he meowed for help.

And, according to news reports, Jerry's owner, Anne Shewring, was not shocked at the situation: "Most cats would have eaten them, but Jerry's a big softie," she said.

Maybe so, but no one's taking any chances: The rescued birds were taken away and released in a nature sanctuary.

BIRD + DOG

Birds of a feather don't necessarily flock together. At least not in the case of one lonely pigeon and a black and white sheepdog named Zoë. After Pretty Bird lost her mate, she and Zoë became inseparable. They slept in Zoë's kennel and when Zoë ate, the pigeon always sat on the edge of her dish. At nap time, they could be found asleep on the lawn with Zoë resting her paw on Pretty Bird, who lay snoozing contentedly underneath. And on several occasions, the two lovebirds have even been heard talking with each other in strange grunts and chirps.

DUMB JOKES

Need a good laugh? Well, you might like these anyway.

Q: What do you get when you cross a skunk with a boomerang?
A: A smell you can't get rid of.

Q: What do you call a fly that has no wings?
A: A walk.

Q: What's the difference between roast beef and pea soup?
A: Anyone can roast beef.

Did you hear the one about the roof? Never mind. It's over your head.

A man was telling his neighbor, "I just bought a new state-of-the-art hearing aid. It cost me a thousand dollars."

"Really," said the neighbor. "What kind is it?"

"Twelve thirty."

Q: What did the farmer count his cattle with?
A: A cowculator.

Did you hear about the new pirate movie? It's rated Arghhhhhhh.

Q: What do you call a hippie's wife?
A: Mississippi.

Census taker: "How many children do you have?"
Lady: "Four."
Census taker: "May I have their names, please?"
Lady: "Eenie, Meenie, Minie…and George."
Census taker: "Why did you name your fourth child George?"
Lady: "Because we didn't want any Moe."

Q: What do you do every 2 to 10 seconds?   A: Blink.

HOW TO BECOME A MILLIONAIRE IN 30 DAYS

Do you have to work to make money? Not according to our friend Jess Braillier, who showed us this get-rich-quick scheme.

EASY STREET
Want to make an easy $10 million and change? Hey, who doesn't? But how? Be an NBA star? Be a movie star? Create an Internet start-up? Well, you could try those ways... or you could try this perfectly legal scam.

First, find someone with lots of money (A wealthy relative is a logical target). Offer to do some daily chore for them, like picking up after the dog or taking out the garbage. But don't act too excited, or you'll risk raising their suspicions.

WHAT TO DO
Now tell Uncle Billfold or Aunt Moneybags that for this daily chore, you'll charge just 1¢ the first day. And that each day after that, you'll charge just twice as much as the day before. Your average sucker will figure, "Let's see, that's one cent the first day, two cents the

As of 2000, more people live in California than live in any other state (34,501,130).

next day, and, uh, only four cents the next day—hey, sure, it's a deal."

Congratulations! You've just done it. In 30 days, you'll be a multimillionaire. Check it out!

Day 1,	you earn $0.01
Day 2,	you earn $0.02
Day 3,	you earn $0.04
Day 4,	you earn $0.08
Day 5,	you earn $0.16
Day 6,	you earn $0.32
Day 7,	you earn $0.64
Day 8,	you earn $1.28
Day 9,	you earn $2.56
Day 10,	you earn $5.12
Day 11,	you earn $10.24
Day 12,	you earn $20.48
Day 13,	you earn $40.96
Day 14,	you earn $81.92
Day 15,	you earn $163.84
Day 16,	you earn $327.68
Day 17,	you earn $655.36
Day 18,	you earn $1,310.72
Day 19,	you earn $2,621.44

Day 20, you earn $5,242.88

Day 21,
    you earn $10,485.76

Day 22,
    you earn $20,971.52

Day 23,
    you earn $41,943.04

Day 24,
    you earn $83,886.08

Day 25,
    you earn $167,772.16

Day 26,
    you earn $335,544.32

Day 27,
    you earn $671,088.64

Day 28,
    you earn........$1,342,177.28

Day 29,
    you earn........$2,684,354.56

Day 30,
    you earn........$5,368,709.12

Grand total for all 30 days: $10,737,418.24!
(*Don't spend it all in one place.*)

Snails have teeth.

HONESTLY, ABE

Abraham Lincoln, our 16th president, was surprisingly quotable. Here are a few of his better-known sayings.

"The best way to destroy your enemy is to make him your friend."

"God must love the common man, he made so many of them."

"No man is good enough to govern another man without that other's consent."

"No matter how much cats fight, there always seems to be plenty of kittens."

"People who like this sort of thing will find this the sort of thing they like."

"Human action can be modified to some extent, but human nature cannot be changed."

"Those who deny freedom for others deserve it not for themselves."

"The man who is incapable of making a mistake is incapable of anything."

"As I would not be a slave, so I would not be a master. This expresses my idea of democracy."

"The ballot is stronger than the bullet."

"The things I want to know are in books; my best friend is the man who'll get me a book I ain't read."

"The best thing about the future is that it comes only one day at a time."

Abraham Lincoln hated being called "Abe."

TONGUE TWISTERS

Ready for a workout? Try to say each of these three times fast…and pay no attention to the person banging on the bathroom door, asking what's going on in there.

"What ails Alex?" asks Alice.

Ada made a gator hate her, so the gator ate her.

Six sly shavers sheared six shy sheep.

The big bloke bled in the big blue bed.

The bottom of the butter bucket is the buttered bucket bottom.

A well-read redhead.

Wire-rimmed wheels.

Edgar at eight ate eight eggs a day.

Can a flying fish flee far from a free fish fry?

An itchy rich witch.

Pass the pink peas please.

The fickle finger of fate flips fat frogs flat.

Fleas fly from fries.

Some shun summer sunshine.

Mr. Spink thinks the sphinx stinks.

Home run hitter Mark McGwire was originally drafted as a pitcher.

IT'S A TWISTER!

Hopefully you've never seen a tornado...except maybe on TV. And believe us, you don't want to.

ARE WE IN OZ YET?
If you're looking off into the distance and spot a twisting, turning funnel that looks something like an elephant's trunk coming from a very dark cloud—take cover. It's a tornado!

Tornadoes can pop up almost anywhere, but about 800 of them whirl through the U.S. every year. That's more than any other country in the world.

Where's the best place to spot a tornado? Tornado Alley—a flat stretch of prairie on the Great Plains that goes from South Dakota through Oklahoma and all the way down to Texas. The Lone Star State averages about 139 tornadoes a year. One city—Oklahoma City, Oklahoma—has been struck 33 times in the last 90 years!

RECIPE FOR DESTRUCTION
Tornadoes are usually created by strong thunderstorms. When a large mass of warm air meets a large mass of cold air, you've got the ingredients for a "twister." They can be small—a few feet wide and 10 feet tall—or huge—nearly five miles tall and a mile wide. But they're always destructive and dangerous.

Some tornadoes touch down and race across the land, mowing down everything in their path. Others skip around from place to place, completely destroying one house on a street but not even touching the house next door.

MORE POWERFUL THAN A LOCOMOTIVE

Tornado winds blow the hardest of any winds on Earth—more than 300 miles an hour! Some people say a tornado sounds like a jet taking off; others say it sounds like the buzzing of a million bees. Some have compared it to the sound of a speeding train. And speaking of trains, tornado winds are strong enough to lift a train right off the ground. In 1931 a Minnesota tornado hoisted an 83-ton passenger train filled with 117 people into the air and plunked it down 80 feet from the tracks.

Remember the scene in *The Wizard of Oz* when a twister lifts Dorothy's house high into the air? Could that *really* happen? Well, they might not take you over the rainbow, but tornadoes have been known to lift whole houses right off their foundations.

TAKE COVER!

If you live in Tornado Alley, the time to be watching the skies is late March through late June. If the sky has turned black, with clouds hovering near the ground and a big thunderstorm underway, run for the

See for yourself: the opposite sides of a dice cube always add up to seven.

storm cellar. If you don't have a storm cellar, go to the center of the house and get in a closet or bathroom.

One woman in Oklahoma saw a twister coming down her street and grabbed her two teenage kids and their dog and hopped into the bathtub. Then they covered their heads with a mattress. First they heard a sound like a runaway freight train, then electrical explosions as wires were ripped from the walls. Finally they heard the sound of rain beating down on their mattress. When they peeked out from under the mattress, they found the entire house was gone. The only thing left standing was the bathtub with one mom, two kids, and a dog.

TORNADO TRICKS

• On June 23, 1944, a tornado blew all the water out of the West Fork River in West Virginia…and then it put it back.

• A tornado in Pennsylvania took the walls off several houses…but left the furniture.

*　　*　　*

DOLLAR FACTS

• It costs the United States government 7.8¢ to make a 50¢ coin.

• It costs 3¢ to make a $1 bill.

• In an emergency, you can use a $1 bill to measure length. It's 6.125 inches long, roughly half a foot.

Mr. Rogers is an ordained minister.

MYTHICAL CREATURES

Before TV, before Gameboy and the Nintendo GameCube, even before books—we had storytellers. The best stories were great adventures with great heroes fighting (and defeating) vicious beasts. And when lions and tigers got too predictable, the ancient storytellers made up new monsters. Here are some mythical creatures you'd NEVER want to meet...

Creature: Manticore
Where It's From: India
Creature's Features: *Manticore* actually means "man-eater," so unless you want to be this creature's lunch, avoid the jungles of India. The Manticore has the head of a man, the body of a lion, and a spiked scorpion's tail. With three rows of teeth and blood-red eyes, he is not a pretty sight. But if you do see him, don't try to run—he can jump great distances and can actually shoot the spines of his tail like arrows. Before he sits down to eat, the Manticore likes to challenge his prey with riddles. If he asks you, in his flutelike voice, what is his favorite food, answer, "A manwich."

Creature: Hydra
Where It's From: Greece
Creature's Features: The *Hydra* is a dragon—but it's no ordinary dragon. It has nine heads, and if you cut

one off, three more grow in its place. According to legend, the Hydra guarded the golden apples on an island at the end of the world. One bite of these apples would give a mortal knowledge that only the gods possessed. The hero Hercules was sent to slay the dragon and steal the apples. He knew he couldn't cut off the Hydra's heads so he *burned* them off, one by one. Now *that's* using your head!

Creature: Chimera
Where It's From: Lycia (ancient Turkey)
Creature's Features: What do you get when you combine a lion, a goat, and a snake? A *Chimera*. This three-headed beast is particularly nasty—it kills its victims by vomiting fire on them and then snacking on their charbroiled remains. The Greek hero Bellerophon killed a Chimera with the help of his winged horse, Pegasus. The Chimera is such an unlikely creature that the word has come to mean "an impossible dream."

Creature: Hippocampus
Where It's From: Greece
Creature's Features: Whenever the sea god Neptune feels like going for a ride, he whistles for his *Hippocampus* and off they gallop across the ocean. This sea creature with the head of a horse and the body of a fish likes to frolic in the foam of sea waves. And speaking of horses, the name *hippocampus* is the official name of that cute little ocean creature—the sea horse.

Chocolate contains vanilla...but vanilla contains no chocolate.

COOL CARTOONS

*You've seen them on TV, but do you
know where they came from?*

SPONGEBOB SQUAREPANTS

What would you expect from a marine biologist who studied animation in college? A cartoon about a wacky talking sponge named Sponge Boy, of course. Sponge Boy? That's what Stephen Hillenburg was going to call his creation…until he found out that someone already owned that name. So he changed it to Sponge-*bob*, which, he says, is much funnier, anyway. Spongebob first appeared on Nickelodeon in April 1999.

DEXTER'S LABORATORY

Dexter started out as a student film by Genndy Tartakovsky, a Russian immigrant who came to the U.S. when he was seven and learned English by watching TV—mostly cartoons. Dexter is modeled on Genndy's older brother Alex. So is Dexter's enemy, Dee-Dee.

THE POWERPUFF GIRLS

The PowerPuff Girls were created in 1998 by animator Craig McCracken, who used to work on *Dexter's Laboratory*. "I wanted to do something of my own—a superhero show," says McCracken, "But I didn't want to just cast strong, muscley guys…so I drew these three little girls, and I thought, 'Oh, wait, this is cool—little cute girls in a really tough environment.'"

What's the Roman numeral for 999? CMXCIX. For 1,000? M.

AMAZING KIDS

*Kids are capable of amazing feats of daring and skill.
Here's a story that proves that you don't have to wait
until you're grown up to attempt the "impossible."*

AMERICA'S BEST GIRL

In 1926 a 19-year-old championship swimmer from New York City named Trudy Ederle decided to take on a new challenge: swimming the English Channel.

Now, the English Channel is not just a little waterway. It's a 21-mile-wide stretch of freezing-cold, choppy sea separating England from France. High winds, powerful undertows, stinging jellyfish, and huge ships are just a few of the dangers a swimmer encounters while trying to cross it. That's why it's considered the ultimate test of a swimmer's endurance.

Trudy knew that hundreds of men and women had tried to swim the channel, and hundreds had failed. Only five swimmers had ever made it to the other side—and all of them were men.

A NEW SUIT

In the 1920s, women who wanted to swim had to wear heavy woolen swim dresses, which made it nearly impossible to swim any distance without sinking. Trudy wanted to give herself the best shot at making it across the Channel, so she wore a sleek silk tanksuit. She also

---

Count 'em yourself (carefully!): Cats have 24 whiskers, 12 on each side of their face.

wore three layers of protective grease: olive oil, lanolin, and lard mixed with petroleum jelly. That not only made her slip through the water faster but also helped to keep her warm.

Trudy began her swim at 7:09 in the morning on August 6. Her father, her coach, and a few reporters followed her in a boat. To keep her spirits up, her dad took along a Victrola (a 1920s version of a "boombox" that you wound up by hand) and played Trudy's favorite songs: "Yes, We Have No Bananas" and "Let Me Call You Sweetheart."

Twelve hours into the swim, the waves got so rough that everyone in the boat was throwing up. The others begged Trudy to quit, but she wouldn't give up. Waves hammered her head with every stroke, so much so that she later lost most of her hearing as a result. But Trudy swam on, fighting the current, the cold, and the nausea.

MADE IT!

Fourteen hours, thirty-one minutes later, at 9:40 p.m., she walked out of the surf onto the French shore. Not only was Trudy Ederle the first woman to swim the English Channel, but she had beaten the men's record by two hours. When reporters asked her how she felt, Trudy replied, "Wet!"

With her record swim, Trudy Ederle became the most famous teenager in the world. President Calvin Coolidge named her "America's Best Girl."

THE BIRTH OF THE SIMPSONS

It may be the most popular primetime cartoon in history. But how did such an outrageous show make it onto the air in the first place? Read on.

OFF THE WALL

In the mid-1980s, producer James L. Brooks was developing a comedy series called *The Tracey Ullman Show* for the brand-new Fox TV network. Ullman was immensely popular in England…but Brooks wasn't sure her humor would play well in the United States. He figured that inserting short cartoon segments between her comedy sketches might help keep the show interesting to American audiences.

Brooks was a fan of cartoonist Matt Groening (pronounced *Graining*), whose weekly cartoon strip "Life in Hell" runs in more than 200 newspapers. He had a Groening poster in his office and one day he remarked to an assistant, "We should get this guy and have him animate for us."

LOST IN SPACE

So Fox officials approached Groening about an animated version of the comic strip and making its characters—two humans named Akbar and Jeff and three rabbits named Binky, Sheba, and Bongo—part of the show. At first, Groening agreed. Then he ran into a problem: "Fox told me, 'We must own the characters and the marketing rights.'"

Groening was making a pretty good living licensing the characters for calendars, mugs, and T-shirts, and didn't want to give it up. But rather than walk away from Fox's offer, he came up with another idea. He dashed off a short story based on his real-life family—Homer and Marge (his parents); Lisa and Maggie (his sisters); and an autobiographical character named Bart (the word "brat" rearranged). He proposed using them instead of the "Life in Hell" characters, and Fox agreed to give it a try.

A NEW FAMILY

As Groening developed these characters for TV, they began to lose their resemblance to his real family. (His father, for example, isn't bald, and his mother no longer wears "big hair.") He changed their last name to the all-American sounding "Simpson" and fashioned them after old sitcom characters.

"I used to spend hours in front of a TV watching family situation comedies," he said in 1990. "What is *The Simpsons* but a hallucination of the sitcom?"

The original cartoons were only 15 to 20 seconds long, so Bart was the only well-developed character. "He was a deviant," Groening says. Homer's voice was an impersonation of actor Walter Matthau, Lisa was supposed to be a "female Bart," and Marge and Maggie weren't much more than backdrops for the other characters.

FIRST LOOK

The *Tracey Ullman Show* debuted in 1987. Critics loved it, but ratings were terrible. Despite this, *The Simpsons* attracted a huge cult following, and Fox responded by increasing the length of the cartoons to 90 seconds. Then they introduced a line of *Simpsons* T-shirts, posters, and other items to cash in on the fad.

But the biggest boost to *The Simpsons*'s popularity came from a candy bar company. The makers of Butterfinger and Baby Ruth licensed the Simpson characters for their ads—which aired on network TV. So kids who'd never heard of the *Tracey Ullman Show* finally got a glimpse of Bart and his family. Their popularity grew.

ON THEIR OWN

In 1988 Fox decided to spin *The Simpsons* off into a separate show. The first episode aired on January 13, 1990 and earned the second-highest ratings in its time slot—pretty impressive when you consider that Fox didn't have as many affiliates around the country as ABC, CBS, or NBC. By June it went all the way to #3 for *all* time slots. *The Simpsons* went on to become Fox's highest-rated show and helped make Fox the fourth major TV network.

*　　*　　*

"The way people respond to the show is fantastic. You should see the fan mail. Kids send in their pictures of Bart beating up other cartoon characters."

—*Matt Groening*

LIGHTNIN' ROY: THE MAN WHO WOULD NOT DIE

Here's an electrifying tale—shocking…but true.

Roy Sullivan, a forest ranger from Waynesboro, Virginia, was struck by lightning seven different times between 1942 and 1977.

1. The first time he lost his big toenail.

2. The second strike burned off his eyebrows.

3. The third bolt burned him on his left shoulder.

4. When his hair caught on fire after the fourth strike, he started carrying a bucket of water around with him just in case it happened again.

5. It happened again. His hair was set on fire by a fifth blast, which also knocked him out of his car.

6. He hurt his ankle on the sixth strike.

7. The seventh put him in the hospital, having burned his stomach and chest.

Poor Roy could never figure out why lightning was drawn to him, and neither could anyone else. Interesting fact: Roy claimed he could actually see the bolts as they headed for him.

Fish cough.

BATHROOM LORE

It seems appropriate to include a little history of the room you may be sitting in right now.

EARLY BATHROOM HISTORY

- The idea of a separate room for the disposal of bodily wastes goes back at least 10,000 years (to 8000 B.C.). On Orkney, an island off the coast of Scotland, the inhabitants, who lived in stone huts, even created a sewer system that carried the waste directly into a nearby stream.
- Bathtubs dating back to 2000 B.C. have been found on the Mediterranean island of Crete.
- Around 1500 B.C., some upper-class Egyptians had hot and cold running water; it came into their homes through a system of copper pipes.
- The ancient Romans took bathing very seriously, building public bathhouses wherever they settled. Some Roman bathhouses had massage salons, food and wine, gardens, and in at least one case, a public library.

A STEP BACKWARD

- As Christianity became increasingly widespread in Europe, techniques of plumbing and waste disposal—and cleanliness—were forgotten.
- For hundreds of years, people in Europe basically stopped washing their bodies, in large part because nudity—even for reasons of health or hygiene—was

---

The London Bridge has never fallen down.

regarded as sinful by the Church.

• Upper-class citizens tried to cover up the inevitable body odors with perfume, but the rest of the population had to endure the disgusting smells of filth.

CHAMBER POTS AND STREET ETIQUETTE

• Until the early 1800s, Europeans relieved themselves in outhouses, streets, alleys, and anywhere else they happened to feel like it.

• It was so common to relieve oneself in public that people were concerned about how to behave if they noticed acquaintances "urinating or defecating" on the street. Proper etiquette: Act like you don't see them.

• Chamber pots were used inside at night or when it was cold outside. Their contents were supposed to be picked up once a day by a "waste man." But frequently, the chamber pot was dumped out a window at night, which made it dangerous to go strolling in the evening.

A WELCOME CHANGE

• In the 1830s, an outbreak of cholera in London finally convinced the government to improve public sanitation. Over the next 50 years, the British built new public facilities that set an example for the rest of the world to follow.

• The bathroom we know today—with a combination toilet and bath—didn't exist until the 1850s.

• Until then, the term *bathroom* meant, literally, a room with a bathtub in it.

Whales dream.

A FOOD IS BORN

*These brand names are fairly common, but have
you ever wondered where they come from?
Doesn't matter. We'll tell you anyway.*

CAMPBELL'S SOUP

Arthur and John Dorrance took over the Campbell canning company when founder Joseph Campbell retired in 1894. A few years later, they perfected a method of condensing tomato soup—which made it cheaper to package and ship—but they couldn't decide on a design for the label. One day, company employee Herberton L. Williams went to a football game between Cornell and the University of Pennsylvania. Impressed with Cornell's red-and-white uniforms, he suggested they use those colors on the soup label. They did.

LOG CABIN SYRUP

Invented in 1887 by P. J. Towle, a St. Paul, Minnesota, grocer who wanted to combine the flavor of maple syrup with the affordability of sugar syrup. He planned to name it after his boyhood hero, Abraham Lincoln, but there were already so many Lincoln products that he named it after the president's birthplace instead.

PEPPERIDGE FARM

One of Margaret Rudkin's sons suffered from severe asthma, and his condition became worse when he ate

---

Q: What's a *pandiculation*?   A: That's what doctors call a yawn.

processed food. Unable to find a bread that didn't make him ill, she started baking her own—a stone-ground whole wheat bread. One day in 1935, she brought a loaf to the boy's doctor who liked it so much he began recommending it to others. After building up a small business selling to local asthmatics, she expanded her business and named her company after the family farm in Connecticut…Pepperidge Farm.

CELESTIAL SEASONINGS

In 1969, four hippies spent their time roaming the Rocky Mountains gathering herbs for their own home-made tea. They got so good at it that they decided to sell herbs to local health-food stores. They bankrolled the operation by selling an old Volkswagen and named the company after one of the four, whose "cosmic" name was Celestial. Today, Celestial Seasonings is the largest herbal tea company on Earth.

RAGÚ SPAGHETTI SAUCE

When Giovanni and Assunta Cantisano stepped off the boat in New York City at the turn of the 20th century, they brought with them a few belongings…and the family recipe for spaghetti sauce. Giovanni opened a store selling Italian wine and foods. He thought he might be able to make a little extra money selling the family's spaghetti sauce there, so in 1937 he put some in Mason jars and stocked his shelves with it. He never bothered to name it—he just called it Ragú, the Italian word for "sauce."

Your thighbones (one in each leg) are the longest bones in your body.

PRESIDENTIAL Q & A

Which U.S. presidents saw a UFO? Why did Lincoln grow a beard? Take this quiz and find out.

Q: Who was the first presidential wife to be called "First Lady"?
A: Lucy Ware Hayes, the wife of Rutherford B. Hayes. And because she banned liquor from the White House, she was also known as "Lemonade Lucy."

Q: How many U.S. presidents were only children?
A: So far, no president has been an only child.

Q: Who was the first president to visit a foreign country while in office?
A: Theodore Roosevelt. He visited Panama in 1906. The 25th president was also the first president to ride in an automobile, fly in an airplane, and dive in a submarine.

Q: Who was the shortest U.S. president?
A: James Madison—he was only 5'4" tall and weighed less than 100 pounds.

Q: What two U.S. presidents claim to have seen a UFO?
A: Jimmy Carter and Ronald Reagan (it was before they became presidents).

Q: In 1841 President William Henry Harrison died in office. What was Vice President John Tyler doing when

The only common English word that ends with the letters "mt" is *dreamt.*

he was told that he had just become president?

A: He was on his knees playing marbles.

Q: What common social custom was banned from the White House during the administration of James K. Polk (1845–1849)?

A: Dancing. Also banned: card-playing and alcoholic beverages.

Q: Why did Abraham Lincoln grow a beard?

A: Because a little girl wrote him a letter telling him that he would look more handsome that way.

Q: What White House tradition was started by President Carter's daughter, Amy?

A: Amy Carter was nine years old when her family moved to the White House. As part of a school project, she labeled all of the trees on the grounds. Her father liked the idea and made it official. Now all the White House trees have labels with their common and Latin name, as well as information about how they got there.

Q: Who was the oldest man ever elected U.S. president?

A: Ronald Reagan was 73 when he was elected in 1984.

Q: Bill Clinton was elected president in 1992. But that wasn't his first encounter with presidential greatness. What was?

A: In 1962 seventeen-year-old Bill Clinton met President John F. Kennedy and decided that he, too, wanted to be president some day.

Say cheese: An estimated 2,700 photographs are taken every second.

CARNIVAL TRICKS

*Do the booths at carnivals and traveling circuses seem rigged
to you? Well, many of them are. Here are some booths
to look out for—and some tips on how to beat them.*

The Booth: "Ring a Bottle"
    The Object: Throw a ring over the neck of a
    soft-drink bottle from about five feet away.
How It's Rigged: The game isn't rigged, but it
doesn't have to be—it's almost impossible to win.

• In 1978 researchers tossed 7,000 rings at a
grouping of 100 bottles. They recorded 12
wins—an average of one shot in every 583
throws. What's more, all of the 12 winning
tosses were *bounced* on; not a single aimed
shot had gone over the bottles. In fact, the
light, plastic rings wouldn't stay on the bottles even if dropped from a height of three
inches directly over the neck of the bottle.
How to Win: The only way to win is to throw two
rings over a bottle neck at the same time…but carnival
operators usually won't let you throw more than one at
a time.

The Booth: "The Milk Can"
The Object: Toss a softball into a 10-gallon milk can.
How It's Rigged: Most carnival cans aren't ordinary
dairy cans. For the midway game, an extra piece of steel

is attached to the rim of the can, reducing the size of
the opening from 6$\frac{1}{2}$ inches down to 4$\frac{3}{8}$ inches.

How to Win:

• Give the ball a backspin and try to hit the back edge
of the can.

• Another way: Toss the ball as high as you can, so that
it drops straight into the hole. This isn't always easy:
operators often hang prizes from the rafters of the booth
to make high tosses difficult.

The Booth: "The Bushel Basket"

The Object: Toss softballs into a bushel basket from a
distance of about six feet.

How It's Rigged: The bottom of the basket is connected to the baseboard in such a
way that it has a lot of spring to
it, so the ball will usually bounce
out.

• Some carnies use a heavier
ball when demonstrating the
game or to give to players for a
practice shot. Then, when play
begins, they switch to a lighter ball that's harder to keep
in the basket.

How to Win:

• Ask to use the same ball the carny used.

• The best throw is to aim high, and aim for the lip or
the sides of the basket. The worst place to put the ball
is directly on the bottom of the basket.

FELINE FACTS

*Cats are America's most popular pet. Here are
five things you may not know about them.*

THE INSIDE POOP

Most domestic cats bury their feces—but in the wild, only timid cats do. This leads researchers to believe that domestic cats actually see themselves as submissive members of their human families.

FAMILY FLAVOR

Does your cat lick its fur clean after it rubs against you? That's its way of "tasting" you—becoming familiar with the taste and scent of the people in its life.

CAT AND MOUSE

Why do cats play "cat and mouse" with their victims? Experts say it's because they're not hungry. Wild cats, who eat only the food they catch, rarely, if ever, do it.

PURR-FECT

Do cats purr because they're happy? Probably not— even sick cats purr. Some researchers think purring is a sign that the cat is receptive to "social interaction."

WHISKED AWAY

A cat's whiskers are sensitive to the air currents around solid objects, such as furniture and trees. That helps it "see" in the dark, especially when it's hunting at night.

THE FIRST...

*It might not have occurred to you, but there's a first time
for everything. Even everyday items have an origin.
Here are a few fascinating firsts from the BRI files.*

BICYCLE
The first practical bike was invented in 1839
by an English blacksmith named Kirkpatrick
Macmillan. It weighed 57 pounds, had iron wheels and
a curved wooden frame, and a horse's head was carved
into the front.

VENDING MACHINE

The first successful automatic vending machine was
set up at a subway station in London in 1883. It sold
postcards. Within a few years, vending machines were
selling eggs, perfume, handkerchiefs, condensed milk,
cough drops, sugar, and accident insurance.

DENTAL DRILL

The first record of a dental drill was described in 1728
by French dental surgeon Pierre Fauchard, in his book
Le Chirurgien-Dentiste. The device was operated by
twisting it with your fingers in alternate directions.

CASH REGISTER

Patented by Ohio saloon owner James J. Ritty on
November 4, 1879. Ritty invented the cash register to

Mr. Potatohead was the first toy advertised on TV. The year: 1952.

cut down on the constant stealing by his bartenders.

AIRLINE FOOD

The first attempt at serving food in an airplane was made by Handley Page Transport. They offered packed lunchboxes on their London–Paris flights beginning October 11, 1919. The first hot meal was served by the French airline Air Union—a five-course lunch with a choice of wines—in 1925.

BREAKFAST CEREAL

Shredded Wheat was the first ready-to-eat cereal ever made. It was produced by Henry D. Perky, a lawyer from Denver, Colorado, in 1893. Perky suffered from chronic indigestion and thought this cereal would cure him.

CIRCUS

Established in 1769 by ex-cavalryman Philip Astley. He sold a diamond ring he'd found and used the money to open a one-ring circus in London to exhibit his horse-back-riding skills. There was no tent, no seats, and no admission was charged—but a collection was taken up after every performance.

POTATO CHIPS

First prepared in 1853 at the Moon Lake House Hotel, in Saratoga Springs, New York, by chef George Crum, when a customer kept sending back his french fries, asking the chef to make them thinner.

A HISTORY OF THE YO-YO, PART I

What's it like being in the yo-yo business? They say it has its ups and downs. Here's a brief history of one of the world's most popular toys.

WHODUNNIT?

• The yo-yo is believed to be the second oldest toy in the world, after dolls. No one knows for sure when or where it was invented: some think China; others think the Philippines.

• Most yo-yo experts agree that a version of the toy was used as a weapon in the Philippines as far back as prehistoric times. Hunters wrapped 20-foot leather straps around heavy pieces of flint and hurled the rock at their prey. If a hunter missed, he could pull the rock back and try again. (The name *yo-yo* comes from a Filipino expression meaning "come come.")

• Even after it was no longer used as a weapon, the yo-yo remained an important part of Filipino culture: people used yo-yo contests to settle arguments. Yo-yoing became the national pastime of the islands. "To this day," says one game historian, "young, rural Filipinos spend weeks carving their own custom yo-yos out of rare wood or water buffalo horn."

Turn to page 114.

YO-YOS IN EUROPE

• The Greeks played with yo-yos as far back as 500 B.C. There are ancient yo-yos made out of clay on display in the Museum of Athens.

• In the 1700s, the yo-yo was introduced into Europe and became popular with the upper classes. In England, the yo-yo was known as the *bandalore*, *quiz*, or *Prince of Wales's toy*.

COMING TO AMERICA

"Bandalores" appeared in the United States in the 19th century. For about 100 years, they occasionally popped up as local fads…then faded in popularity each time. They never disappeared completely but didn't become really popular until the 1920s.

Enter Donald Duncan. The turning point for the yo-yo in America came in 1928, when a businessman named Donald Duncan happened to see Pedro Flores, owner of the Flores Yo-Yo Corporation, demonstrating yo-yos in front of his store. Duncan was impressed with the huge crowds that had gathered to watch. He figured a mass-produced yo-yo could make a lot of money—so in 1929 he and Flores began manufacturing yo-yos on a larger scale. A year later, Duncan bought Flores's share of the company and renamed it after himself.

Spin Control. That's not all he did—he also changed the design of the yo-

yo. The yo-yos Duncan manufactured in 1929 had an important new feature: The string was looped loosely around the axle (the center post between the two halves of the yo-yo). This allowed a Duncan Yo-Yo to "sleep," which meant it could spin freely at the end of the string. And that meant a Duncan Yo-Yo could perform an endless number of tricks.

He started out with just one model—the O-Boy Yo-Yo Top—but by the early 1930s had a whole line of yo-yo products…and a trademark on the name yo-yo. So legally, his company was the only one in the United States that could call its toy a yo-yo.

Owning the name "yo-yo" helped Duncan build a huge toy empire and turn the yo-yo into a national craze. But what goes up, must come down…and up…and down…

Turn to page 196 for part II of the story.

*   *   *

KIDS' ADVICE TO OTHER KIDS

"Never trust a dog to watch your food."
—**Patrick, age 10**

"When your dad is mad and asks you, 'Do I look stupid?' don't answer."
—**Hannah, age 9**

"Never tell your mom her diet's not working."
—**Michael, age 14**

Hawaii is the only U.S. state that was once a kingdom.

SPORTS SHORTS

Impress your friends with some of these little-known facts from the wild world of sports.

Pinned. Bowling was originally played with nine pins. An anti-gambling law was passed in colonial Connecticut more than 150 years ago making "bowling at nine pins" illegal. So to get around the law, bowlers added a pin. And it's been 10 pins ever since.

Population Boom. When the University of Nebraska Cornhuskers play a home football game, the stadium becomes the state's third largest city.

Quick Quiz: What do golf, croquet, lacrosse, rugby, cricket, water skiing, polo, and tug-of-war all have in common? **Answer:** They used to be Olympic sports, but aren't any more.

Amazing Coincidence. In 1963 the winners of the Most Valuable Player award in pro football, basketball, and baseball (National *and* American Leagues) all wore number 32. They were Jim Brown (NFL), Elgin Baylor (NBA), Sandy Koufax (National League), and Elston Howard (American League).

Like Father, Like Son. On September 14, 1990 Ken Griffey, Sr. and Ken Griffey, Jr. became the first father and son to hit back-to-back home runs in a Major League Baseball game.

Lemons contain more sugar than strawberries do.

GROSS STUFF

Your body makes all kinds of disgusting goo. Our favorite pick: the stuff that comes out of your nose.

BOOGERS

They're green, they're gooey, and they're gross. Everybody has them. But what exactly is a booger? Basically this little slimeball is the result of your nose protecting your body. Picture this: you take a deep breath and a piece of dust whooshes into your nostrils. That dust particle instantly meets little tiny nose hairs—called *cilia*—which are there to stop the dust from going any farther.

But it doesn't always work, and sometimes the dust gets past the nose hairs. If it does, it will bump into the *mucous membrane*, which has a surface something like a sticky fly strip or piece of masking tape. This membrane makes a gooey liquid called *mucus* that catches and destroys any dust or bacteria trying to invade your body. How? It surrounds the dust or bacteria, and *voila!* You've got a booger. The exact color is determined by what kind of particles came into your nose.

Once the mucus is used up, your body whips up another batch. Your body can make as much as a *quart* of mucus a day. That's equal to four glasses of milk!

> You can pick your friends...
> And you can pick your nose...
> But you can't pick your friend's nose.

More than half of the bones in your body are in your hands and feet.

BUT IT SAYS ON THE LABEL...

Think that you can tell what's in the products you buy by reading the labels? Think again. Here are four examples that show how companies stretch the truth to increase sales.

FRESH IS FROZEN

The Label Says: "This Turkey Never Frozen"

You Assume: It's fresh turkey.

Actually: According to government rules, to be called "fresh," a turkey has to be stored at above 26°F—the freezing point for poultry. But the label still doesn't have to say "frozen" unless it was stored at 0°F (or below). So a company can legally say it was never frozen…even if it was stored at 1°F.

YOUR LAWN OR YOUR LIFE?

The Label Says: "Pesticide Ingredients," then lists them

You Assume: All the ingredients—particularly the toxic ones—are on the list.

Actually: According to a recent study, "over 600 toxic chemicals included in pesticides aren't disclosed on the brand labels." Why not? "Under federal regulations, these chemicals don't have to be listed if they are *inert* ingredients—chemicals that assist in killing bugs or

Lonely parrots can go insane.

weeds, but aren't the active agent of destruction." Why aren't they listed? Pesticide companies say they need to protect trade secrets.

DO IT AGAIN

The Label Says: "Recycled Paper"

You Assume: It's been used by a consumer—as newspaper, office paper, cardboard, etc.—then sent to a recycling center, and turned back into paper.

Actually: The only time you can be sure that's true is if the label says "Post-Consumer." Otherwise, it could be something else. Paper manufacturers dump paper from the mill floor back into the paper pulp... and the government allows them to call this paper "recycled."

DEM BONES

The Label Says: "Chicken Nuggets"

You Assume: It's chicken meat.

Actually: According to the National Consumer League, when convenience foods such as chicken frankfurters, chicken nuggets, and turkey bologna are processed, there's no telling what's in them. "Mechanically deboned poultry may contain bone fragments, marrow, kidneys, skin, and lungs as by-products of the process. These by-products are not listed as ingredients, though, so consumers don't know that they are eating this material.... Labeling requirements allow the poultry industry to hide behind a vague description of product as 'chicken meat.'"

More than 150 Native American languages are still spoken in the United States.

FUN INVENTIONS

A lot of people have ideas for gadgets, games, or extremely cool new toys that just might make a million dollars. But not everyone does something with that idea. Here are some stories of people (including a few kids) who did.

TINKERTOYS

You mean there was something before Legos?
One day Charles Pajeau was watching some kids play with pencils, sticks, and empty spools of thread. That gave him the idea to make a toy that children could put together in lots of different ways. He built the first set in his garage and named it The Thousand Wonder Builder. Then in 1914, he formed a company called the Toy Tinkers Company. When he first tried to sell his toy, nobody was interested. But Pajeau didn't give up.

That Christmas, he got the brilliant idea to dress midgets in elf costumes and have them play with the "Tinkertoys" in a Chicago department store window. Moms and dads loved it. Within the year, he had sold over a million sets! In 1998 the Tinkertoy was voted into the National Toy Hall of Fame.

POPSICLE

Uh-oh. Brain freeze!
The year was 1905. Frank Epperson was 11 years old.

He hadn't planned on becoming an inventor; it just happened. Frank had mixed himself a glass of soda pop from a powdered mix (that's how you did it in those days!), set it down on the back porch, and forgot about it. That night the temperature dropped below freezing.

The next day, Frank found that his glass of soda pop had frozen solid, with the stir stick standing straight up. He grabbed the stick, pulled the frozen pop out of the glass, and *voilà!* Frank had discovered a tasty new treat!

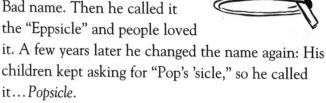

At first, he called it the Epperson Icicle. Good idea. Bad name. Then he called it the "Eppsicle" and people loved it. A few years later he changed the name again: His children kept asking for "Pop's 'sicle," so he called it...*Popsicle*.

FRISBEE

It's a bird! It's a plane! It's a...pie plate?

In the 1940s, college kids at Yale University would toss around their pie plates after dinner just for fun. The pie tins had the name of the baker, Frisbie, embossed on the bottom. But Walter Frederick Morrison didn't know anything about the pie plates when he invented his new toy in the 1950s—a metal disc that he called "The Flying

Saucer." (Walter soon changed the metal to plastic and changed the name to the Pluto Platter.)

It wasn't until Walter sold his flying disc to the Wham-O Toy Company in 1955 that they discovered students on the East Coast already "Frisbie-ing." So they changed the name of the toy to Frisbee (notice the different spelling?) in honor of the original flying pie plates.

Today Frisbee is a national sport. There's Ultimate Frisbee, Frisbee golf, Frisbee championships, and Frisbee dog contests. And yep, it's in the National Toy Hall of Fame, too. Right alongside Monopoly, Barbie, and Play-Doh.

SNOWBOARD

Kowabunga!

In the 1950s, there was the surfboard. Then a few "shredders" wondered what would happen if they attached a pair of rollerskates to a surfboard. Pretty soon they were hanging 10 on the "sidewalk surfer." In the 1960s, a change of wheels, a new design, and a name change turned the skateboard into a national craze.

In 1963, an eighth grader named Tom Sims wondered what would happen if he built a skateboard that could go in the snow. He worked on his new "ski board" in shop class. It looked like a very short, fat ski. Tom tried it out on local hills, and it worked great. He did spins and high-speed turns in the snow. He was stoked!

Youngest inventor in U.S. history: Robert Patch, age 6. He patented a toy truck in 1963.

Tom made more boards, adding foot straps so they would stay on the rider's feet. Fourteen years later, Tom formed a company to manufacture his new invention and became one of the pioneers of "snowboarding."

MONOPOLY

Who wants to be a millionaire?

The stock market crash of 1929 put millions of Americans out of work. One of them was Charles Darrow. He and his friends often sat around the kitchen table, dreaming about what they would do if they had lots of money. That gave Charles an idea. Why not invent a game where people could pretend to be millionaires?

He made a game board using the street names of his favorite town, Atlantic City, New Jersey, cut out cardboard houses and hotels, and typed up title cards for the different "properties." He called this new game Monopoly and invited some friends to play it. Soon they were making (and losing) fortunes in pretend real estate just like the money moguls they read about in the papers. His friends loved the game so much that they asked for their own copies so they could play Monopoly at home. Charles couldn't keep up with the demand. Finally he asked the Parker Brothers game company to sell it. Monopoly soon became the most successful board game in history, and Charles Darrow retired at the age of 46, a genuine millionaire at last.

*   *   *

Random Fact: The official state sport of Maryland is jousting.

The world's longest Monopoly game lasted 660 hours (27.5 days).

FRUIT AND VEGGIE TRIVIA

Amaze your friends with these fascinating facts.

• Top banana: Bananas are the bestselling fruit in America, followed by apples and watermelon.

• The only fruit with its seeds on the *outside* of its skin is the strawberry. (A single strawberry has about 200 seeds.)

• Corn is a member of the grass family. Each ear has an average of 800 kernels.

• Three-quarters of all raisins consumed in the United States are eaten at breakfast.

• Potatoes are the most popular vegetable in the U.S., followed by tomatoes and iceberg lettuce.

• Until the mid-1800s, the most popular and cheapest available beverage (besides water) was apple cider.

• Believe it or not, most fruits contain *some* fat. Most fatty: avocados.

• Trick question: What "vegetable" has no roots, no leaves, no seeds, and is not really a vegetable? Mushrooms. (They're actually fungi.)

• Oranges will not ripen after being picked—but lemons will.

• The temperature inside of a cucumber can be 20 degrees lower than the outside. Cool.

BEWARE: HAUNTED HOUSE

Now, children, listen up—Uncle John would like to tell you some "true" tales of ghosties, ghoulies, and haunted houses.

HAUNTED HOUSE: Glamis Castle, Scotland
GHOST STORY: Tales of secret rooms, bloodstained floors, and deals with the Devil make this place a major hangout for ghosts. This is the famous castle of Shakespeare's *Macbeth*, who brutally murdered King Duncan of Scotland almost 1,000 years ago and stained the castle stones with his blood. That was only the beginning—there have been many evil doings at this Scottish keep. Here are a few:

• One story tells of Earl Beardie, the "Wicked Lord" who played cards with the Devil on a Sunday. The Devil won (big surprise!), and now Earl Beardie's ghost is trapped forever in an eternal card game with You-Know-Who.

• Another tale tells of a room in the castle that held a horrible secret. Word spread that the castle's rightful heir, the son of the Earl of Strathmore, was born deformed. This poor monstrous-looking child was locked away in a secret room, never to see the light of day. Now his ghost wanders the halls.

Q: Who invented swim fins? A: Benjamin Franklin.

- Another ghost who walks the halls of this castle is the "Gray Lady," Lady Janet Douglas, who lived there in the 1500s and who some say was a witch. Look for her in the small chapel where she is often seen praying.

HAUNTED HOUSE: The Haunted Mansion at Disneyworld

GHOST STORY: This famous amusement park mansion is designed to scare people—but it may have a few more ghosts than the Disney Imagineers planned.

- Employees talk about "the man with the cane" who is often seen late at night, especially after closing.

- "The man in a tuxedo" is another spirit who appeared to one employee in the mirror where Doombuggy passengers disembark.

- Finally, there's a legend about a woman who wanted to scatter her young son's ashes inside the Haunted Mansion, but was forbidden by Disney officials. She sneaked the ashes inside and scattered them anyway. But apparently, this was not her son's last wish because many people have seen the ghost of a boy sitting near the exit, crying his eyes out.

Are you afraid of mice? If so, then you have *musophobia*.

MONTHS OF THE YEAR

Here's where the names of the months come from.

JANUARY. Named for the Roman god Janus, a two-faced god who "opened the gates of heaven to let out the morning, and closed them at dusk." Janus was the god of all doors, gates, and other entrances. That's why the opening month of the year was named after him.

FEBRUARY. The Roman "month of purification" got its name from *Februarius*, the Latin word for "purification." February 15 was set aside for the Festival of Februa, in which people repented and made sacrifices to the gods to atone for wrongdoing.

MARCH. Named after Mars, the Roman god of war. The ancient Romans placed great emphasis on wars and conquest, so this was the first month of the year until 46 B.C.

APRIL. No one knows the origin of the name. One theory: It comes from *Aprilis* or *aphrilis*—variations of the name Aphrodite, the Greek goddess of love. Other experts think the month is named after the Latin verb *aperire*, which means "to open." (Most plants open their leaves and buds in April.)

MAY. Some think the month is named after Maia, mother of the god Mercury; others think it was named in honor of the *Majores*, the upper branch of the Roman senate.

JUNE. May have been named in honor of Juno, the wife of Jupiter; or it could have been named after the *Juniores*, the lower branch of the Roman senate.

JULY. Named after Julius Caesar.

AUGUST. Named after Gaius Julius Caesar, heir and nephew of Julius Caesar. The Roman senate gave this Caesar the title of "Augustus," meaning "revered," then honored him further by naming a month after him.

SEPTEMBER. From the Latin word *septem*, which means "seven." September was the seventh month until about the year 700 B.C., when Numa Pompilius, the second Roman king, switched the calendar from 304 days to 355 days.

OCTOBER. From *octo*, the Latin word for "eight," because it was once the eighth month of the year. When Romans changed the calendar, they tried to rename it—Germanicus, Antonius, Faustina, and Hercules—but none of the new names stuck.

NOVEMBER. From *novem*, the Latin word for "nine." November was also referred to as "blood month." Reason: It was the peak season for animal sacrifices.

DECEMBER. From *decem*, the Latin word for "ten." Attempts to rename it Amazonius in honor of the mistress of Emperor Commodus failed.

Big spinner: *Wheel of Fortune's* wheel is 8 feet, 6 inches in diameter.

CELEBRITY QUIZ

Test your knowledge on some little-known facts about well-known celebrities. Answers are on page 279.

1. Natalie Portman of *Star Wars* fame was born in:
a) Beijing, China
b) Islamabad, Pakistan
c) Jerusalem, Israel

2. Tom Cruise learns his lines for a movie by:
a) Listening to them on a tape.
b) Reading them in the bathroom.
c) Having a stand-in act them out for him.

3. Will Smith's rapper name is Fresh Prince. Why "Prince"?
a) His childhood hero was Prince Charles.
b) The family dog was named Prince.
c) Because of his "royal attitude."

4. Which politician was Tommy Lee Jones's roommate in college?
a) Bill Clinton
b) George W. Bush
c) Al Gore

5. His real name is Terry Bollea, but you know him better as:
a) The Rock
b) Hulk Hogan
c) Stone Cold Steve Austin

6. When this actor was five years old, he had to be removed from the set of his first TV show because he was being "too disruptive."
a) Leonardo DiCaprio
b) Michael J. Fox
c) Macaulay Culkin

All-American film star Bruce Willis was born in Germany.

7. This movie star's mother was a popular German opera singer:
a) Sandra Bullock
b) Alicia Silverstone
c) Winona Ryder

8. Keanu Reeves's first name means:
a) "Child of destiny" in Italian
b) "Cool breeze over the mountains" in Hawaiian
c) "Warrior sparrow" in Swahili

9. Haley Joel Osment's favorite animals are:
a) Snakes
b) Turtles
c) Lizards

10. To prepare for fight scenes in *Buffy the Vampire Slayer*, Sarah Michelle Gellar learned this martial art:
a) Jiujitsu
b) Kung fu
c) Tae Kwon Do

11. Jean-Claude Van Damme is well known for being a kickboxer and a bodybuilder, but as a teenager, he was into another physical activity:
a) Ballet dancing
b) Cheerleading
c) Arm wrestling

12. Before he became a movie star, Harrison Ford earned a living as a:
a) Teacher
b) Carpenter
c) Veterinarian

13. Comedian Drew Carey served six years in the:
a) Army
b) Navy
c) Marines

14. Before becoming an actor, *Spider-Man*'s Tobey Maguire wanted to be a:
a) Lawyer
b) Chef
c) Hotel manager

What are *bellysinkers, doorknobs, burl cakes,* and *dunkers*? Four nicknames for donuts.

SLIME IN THE NEWS

Here's proof that fact can be stranger than fiction.

'S NOT WHAT YOU THINK

When the U.S. Marines asked scientists to come up with a non-lethal way of stopping bad guys in their tracks, their thoughts turned to... snot.

In 2001 researchers at San Antonio's Southwest Research Institute announced that they had developed the "Mobility Denial System." What's that? It's a spray-on slime that makes any surface so slippery that nothing can walk, run, or drive across it. Floors, stairs, roads, and even lawns become impassable. And if you spray it on walls—even glass—you can't climb or put a ladder against it.

Billed as "banana skin in a can," it's mostly water, but it has a top-secret ingredient similar to the stuff soft contact lenses are made from.

The milky-white goo can be sprayed from a backpack (covering 2,000 square feet) or a cannon (covering the size of two football fields). And it keeps its slippery properties for about 12 hours. Then it dries out and can be swept up.

The image of a bunch of crooks flailing about in a puddle of Elmer's Glue may sound funny, but...it's snot.

THE 10 WORST SNAKES TO BE BITTEN BY

Here's our list of snakes we'd least like to be trapped in the bathroom with.

1. KING COBRA

The largest poisonous snake in the world. According to many experts, it's also the most dangerous. Its venom is so powerful, it can kill an elephant…which in fact, it has. Adults measure on average 14 feet long (the longest on record is 18 feet). When angered, a king cobra "stands" with its head 5 to 6 feet in the air. This snake is found in southeast Asia, southern China, and India.

2. TAIPAN

There are two taipans. The inland taipan is the most venomous snake in the world, 50 times more toxic than a cobra. Untreated, a person bitten by one of these will die in a matter of minutes. The coastal taipan, though its venom isn't as strong, can be even more dangerous. Why? Because it's bigger—almost ten feet long. And although it's shy, it will strike if it's bothered. So, our advice: If you happen to see one, don't bother it.

3. MAMBA

A black or green snake from Africa. The 10- to 14-foot black mamba, which lives among rocks and in tall grass, is the largest and most feared snake in Africa. It is the world's fastest snake (with bursts of speed of up to 15 mph) and may be the only poisonous snake known to stalk humans. Two drops of black mamba venom can kill a person in 10 minutes. The tree-dwelling green mamba is about half as long...but it's just as deadly.

4. BUSHMASTER

Found mostly in Central America, where it occupies the abandoned burrows of other animals. Particularly dangerous because, when confronted, it attacks people rather than fleeing from them, as most snakes do. Has one-inch fangs and carries enough poison to kill several people. It's the largest poisonous snake in the Americas—8 to 12 feet long.

5. DIAMONDBACK RATTLESNAKE

The name comes from the diamond- or hex-shaped blotches on its skin. Measures anywhere from 3 to 8 feet. Because it's aggressive and abundant, the diamondback gives more serious bites and causes more deaths than any other snake in North America. Its poison can kill a mouse in a few seconds, and a person within an hour.

6. FER-DE-LANCE

Also known as the *terciopelo* (Spanish for "velvet"), it is relatively small (about 4 feet long), but especially dangerous to humans because it's nervous and quick to bite. Its venom spreads through the body and causes internal bleeding. Found in tropical areas of the Americas such as Martinique.

7. TROPICAL RATTLESNAKE

Has venom 10 times more potent than its cousin, the diamondback rattler. This variety is found predominantly in Central and South America.

8. TIGER SNAKE

Named for the yellow stripes covering its 6-foot-long body. Usually feeds on mice, frogs, and rats, but occasionally also dines on Australians. A single dose of venom induces pain, vomiting, and circulatory collapse. Mortality rate from a bite is 40 percent.

9. COMMON COBRA

Also known as the Indian cobra. It's the kind of snake tamed by Indian snake charmers and is normally a shy hunter that eats frogs and rats. However, because it lives in populated areas, it is actually more dangerous than the king cobra. Just one bite has enough venom to kill 30 people. It grows 4 to 5 feet long.

10. JARARACUSSU

An aquatic snake from South America with a devastating bite. Although a bite from one of these water-dwellers isn't necessarily fatal, it will cause blindness and tissue damage.

DREW'S VIEWS

These quotes from actress Drew Barrymore may seem simple, but that's exactly why we like them. They're honest, straightforward... and full of truth.

"Everyone is like a butterfly—they start out ugly and awkward and then morph into someone beautiful and graceful."

"When I lay my head on the pillow at night I can say I was a decent person today. That's when I feel beautiful."

"I don't know anybody whose road has been paved perfectly for them; there are no manuals, you don't know what life has in store for you."

"I believe that everything happens for a reason, but it's important to seek out that reason—that's how we learn."

"If you're going to be alive and on this planet, you have to suck the marrow out of every day and get the most out of it."

"There's something liberating about not pretending. Risk. Dare to embarrass yourself."

"Love is the hardest habit to break, and the most difficult to satisfy."

"It's only through listening that you learn, and I never want to stop learning."

"I think it's nice when people find love, because everyone deserves it."

AMAZING KIDS

*Kids are capable of amazing feats of daring and skill.
Here's another story that proves you don't have to wait
till you're grown up to attempt the "impossible."*

ONE KID CAN MAKE A DIFFERENCE
Six-year-old Ryan Hreljac of Kemptville,
Ontario, came home from school one day in
1998 and said, "Mom, Dad, I need $70 for a well in
Africa!" "That's nice," they said and promptly forgot
about it.

Ryan didn't. That day he had learned that thousands
of African children die every year from drinking con-
taminated water. They needed wells to get good water.
When his teacher added that a well only cost $70,
Ryan got his big idea. He kept asking for $70 until
finally his parents said, "OK, if you're really serious
about this, do some extra chores around the house and
we'll pay you for them." They were certain he'd quickly
lose interest in his project. They were wrong.

DETERMINATION

While his brothers played, Ryan cleaned windows and
vacuumed. And pretty soon he had saved the money.
His mother contacted WaterCan, a Canadian agency
that builds wells in Africa, and Ryan went to give them
the money. That's when he learned that $70 only
bought a small hand pump. A *real* well cost more than

Which contains more iron: an adult's body, or an iron nail? They're about equal.

$2,000. Even with some help from the Canadian government, Ryan would have to come up with 10 times the amount he'd worked so hard to raise. Ryan smiled and said, "I'll just do more chores."

His mom and dad knew it was almost impossible for a six-year-old to raise that much money doing jobs around the house. He needed help. A newspaper reporter agreed to write a story about Ryan. A photographer came out and took pictures. The reporter told Ryan and his family that a big newspaper would run the story. But weeks passed and nothing happened.

Ryan kept right on raising money. And once again, he reached his goal.

A NEW GOAL

WaterCan told Ryan that his well would be dug in Uganda, near the Angolo Elementary School. While thanking Ryan for his contribution, a WaterCan official mentioned that it would take more than a week to drill Ryan's well by hand. If they had a better drill, he said, they could help more people. "How much would that drill cost?" Ryan asked.

"$25,000."

"I'll get you that drill," Ryan said. "I want everyone in Africa to have clean water." He was then seven years old.

His parents were frantic. When was this determined little kid going to realize that there was a limit to what he could do?

Eels can swim backward. Most other fish can't.

POWER OF THE PRESS

Then the article hit the newspapers. Soon the story about Ryan and his well was all over Canada...and the money poured in. Within five months, Ryan raised the $25,000. And the well was dug. He dreamed of being able to see it someday.

SEEING IS BELIEVING

Then some friends of Ryan's family donated their frequent flyer airline miles to get him a ticket to Africa. At last, Ryan would get to see his well. When he arrived, Ugandans lined the road for miles to cheer the Canadian boy who got them their well.

Ryan Hreljac is still at it today. So far, the money he's raised has built more than 30 wells...and saved thousands of lives.

* * *

SPACED-OUT SPORTS

"Three things are bad for you. I can't remember the first two, but doughnuts are the third."
—college football coach, Bill Petersen

"Tony Gwynn was named player of the year for April."
—sportscaster Ralph Kiner

"Noah."
—Barry Bonnel, former Seattle Mariner,
asked to name his all-time favorite Mariner

In Japan, it's considered impolite to show your teeth when you're laughing.

UNMENTIONABLES

Skivvies, briefs, BVDs, undies, panties, drawers—whatever you want to call 'em, they're all the same—underwear.

THE IRON AGE

Some people prefer cotton underwear. Some people think silk feels pretty nice. But can you imagine wearing underwear made out of iron? That's what women in the 1800s did.

Why? Because they wanted to have tiny little waists. And in order to get an hourglass shape, they wore corsets that were stiffened with iron rods. Some were stiffened with whalebone (yes, from the bones of a whale). But whatever was used, it hurt!

Corsets were laced so tight that some women's ribs actually broke. Women often couldn't get enough air into their lungs, so fainting was common. And what did they do about this problem? A smart person would have worn looser underwear. Instead, they invented "fainting couches." This way a woman with too tight a corset had a soft place to land when she passed out from lack of oxygen.

BOOM OR BUST

And speaking of shape changing, underwear has often

Dinosaurs died out 65 million years before the first humans appeared on Earth.

been used to shrink or enlarge other parts of the body. In the 1920s, women wore bust flatteners to make their chests look flat. In the 1950s, "sweater girls" were wearing padded bras to make their chests look big. And believe it or not, you can even buy padded underwear to make your hips look bigger or your bottom look rounder.

LONG JOHNS

Long before boxers and briefs, men wore long underwear. Sometimes called long johns or a union suit, this one-piece item buttoned up the front and had a little drop door that buttoned (and unbuttoned) in the back. They are still worn today as extra protection in cold weather.

MEN IN SKIRTS

In Scotland, men have always worn wool skirts called kilts. Each kilt is made of a plaid fabric that has a design unique to their clan, or family. So the Macdonald kilt has a much different pattern then a Campbell kilt. Prince Charles often wears a Stuart kilt. And you may have seen bagpipers—they always wear kilts. But the big, burning question that people have asked for ages is: "What does a Scotsman wear under his kilt?" The official answer: "Absolutely nothing."

BAD LUCK AT THE OLYMPICS

On page 249 we tell you about some bizarre good luck charms used by various athletes. Maybe these Olympic athletes could have used a rabbit's foot, too.

HORSE OFF COURSE

Olympic gymnasts know that the "horse" in the women's vaulting competition is supposed to be set at 125 centimeters (about four feet) off the floor. That's what they all practice on. But for some reason, the people who installed the horse at the 2000 games in Sydney, Australia, set it at 120 centimeters—about 2 inches too short. So what happened? Several gymnasts misjudged the height and fell. Hardest hurt was the favorite, Russia's Svetlana Khorkina, who missed the landing and was so shaken that later she also fell off the uneven bars.

WATCH THIS!

What if you win an event and no one notices? That's what happened to Frenchman Jules Noël at the 1932 summer games in Los Angeles. His discus throw went farther than anyone else's, but distracted officials were busy watching the pole vault competition. Result: The throw was "unofficial." They apologized and let him throw again, but it fell short of the previous mark. Noël ended up in fourth place—just short of a medal.

Would you like to be an *ethologist?* That's someone who studies animal behavior.

TOO GOOD FOR HIS OWN GOOD

At the 1928 St. Moritz games in Switzerland, Norwegian ski jumper Jacob Tullin Thams had such a strong jump—nine meters (about 30 feet) farther than the next guy—that he flew beyond the hill where skiers were supposed to land. The jump was great, but the flat surface he landed on made him crash. Penalized for style points, the longest jump of the day earned him 28th place in the standings.

WHO'S COUNTING?

The 3,000-meter steeplechase (horse race) at the 1932 games was close as the horses entered the final lap. At least it was supposed to be the final lap. Somehow, the judges had lost count and didn't call the race over until an additional lap had been run. American Joseph McCluskey would have won a silver medal, but was passed on that second "final" lap and only won the bronze.

SOME FRIEND!

South African long-distance runners Christian Gitsham and Kenneth McArthur were good friends. Or so Gitsham thought. They were both leading the field in the marathon in the 1912 Olympics in Stockholm, Sweden, when only two miles from the finish, Gitsham got thirsty. McArthur told Gitsham he would wait while his friend got a drink of water. He didn't. Gitsham lost by almost a minute.

Q: What's a *sternutation*?   A: That's what doctors call a sneeze. (Bless you!)

KNOW YOUR CLOUDS

Some are close to Earth; some tower high in the sky. Some look like puffy cotton balls, some are dark and layered. Take a moment to look up at the sky and see if you recognize these types of clouds.

WHY DO CLOUDS HAVE NAMES?

In 1802 an English druggist named Luke Howard proposed a system of classifying the different types of clouds. His main three categories: *cirrus* (from the Latin word for "curl," or "lock of hair"), *cumulus* (from the Latin word for "heap," or "pile"), and *stratus* (from the Latin word for "layers"). By combining these terms with other terms, such as *nimbus* (from the Latin word for "halo"), he came up with 10 cloud classifications. Since then, the terms have been slightly modified and some additions have been made, but Howard's basic system is still used worldwide 200 years later.

WHAT EXACTLY IS A CLOUD?

Those white fluffy things floating around the sky are actually collections of billions of droplets of water or ice crystals. But not all clouds are the same.

• The white fluffy ones that look like floating sheep or mountains are called **cumulus** clouds. They form when warm moist air rises fast and is cooled fast.

• Light, wispy clouds that look like feathers or curls of hair are called **cirrus** clouds. They are formed very high

---

A good day to spend time with friends: June 11 is National Cheer Up the Lonely Day.

in the sky where the air is very cold. They contain only ice crystals.

- **Nimbostratus** clouds are dark and hang low in the sky. These are the true rain (and snow) clouds. Sheets of rain from these clouds often reach the ground.

- **Cumulonimbus** clouds are white fluffy clouds with dark bottoms. Winds often flatten out their tops. These storm clouds make lightning and thunder. They also give us tornadoes.

- If it seems like you're looking at the sun through frosted glass, you're probably seeing **altostratus** clouds. They appear to be big sheets of gray or blue in the sky.

- **Stratus** clouds are thick and layered. These clouds hang low and heavy, like fog, and cover a large area. They are often a dull gray color.

- Ever look up into the sky and think you're looking at a weird UFO, or an upside-down hat? That's what **lenticular** clouds look like. They don't move like other clouds and sometimes hover in one place for hours. There are some people who think that these clouds actually hide spaceships!

*   *   *

DUMB CROOKS

A pair of would-be robbers stormed into a record shop waving handguns. The first robber shouted, "Nobody move!" When his partner moved, the startled first bandit shot him. Both were arrested.

Turn to page 83.

MEET DR. SEUSS

Say hello to Dr. Seuss, a rhymer of rhymes both tight and loose.
A BRI favorite he really is; the following story is really his.

V ITAL STATS
Real Name: Theodor Seuss Geisel
Born: March 2, 1904
Died: September 25, 1991, age 87

• Although married twice, he never had any children. His slogan: "You have 'em, I'll amuse 'em."

• He adopted "Seuss" as his writing name while attending Dartmouth College. The reason: He was caught with a half-pint of gin in his room and was told to resign as editor of the college humor magazine as punishment. Instead, he just stopped using Geisel as his byline.

• Years later, he added "Dr." to his name "to sound more scientific." But he didn't officially become a doctor until 1956, when Dartmouth gave him an honorary doctorate.

HOW HE GOT STARTED

He was working as an artist for an advertising agency in New York in 1936 when he wrote *To Think That I Saw It on Mulberry Street*. It was turned down by 27 publishers. Said Seuss: "The excuse I got for all those rejections was that there was nothing on the market quite like it, so they didn't know whether it would sell." Vanguard Press finally picked it up in 1937, and it was an immediate success. So he quit the ad agency and began writing kids' books full-time.

CAREER STATS

Accomplishments: He wrote 48 books, selling more than 100 million copies in 20 languages. (Including four of the bestselling hardcover children's books of all time: *The Cat in the Hat*, *Green Eggs and Ham*, *Hop on Pop*, and *One Fish, Two Fish, Red Fish, Blue Fish*.)

• As a filmmaker, he won three Oscars: two for documentaries made in the 1940s, and one in 1951 for animation (*Gerald McBoing-Boing*). By that time, he had written four kids' books and turned down Hollywood screenplay offers in order to keep writing them.

• In 1984 he won the Pulitzer Prize for his contribution to children's literature.

Flops: Only one—he wrote a novel called *The Seven Lady Godivas*, which was, according to one critic, "an utterly ridiculous retelling of the story of Lady Godiva" that was first published in 1937 and republished 40 years later. But the book bombed in 1977, too.

HOW HE GOT HIS IDEAS

"The most-asked question of any successful author," Seuss said in 1989, "is 'How do you get your ideas for books?'" Over the years he did reveal a number of his inspirations:

Horton Hatches the Egg

"Sometimes you have luck when you are doodling. One

A *squawk* is when you squall (yell) and squeak at the same time.

day I was drawing some trees. Then I began drawing elephants. I had a window open, and the wind blew the elephant on top of the tree; I looked at it and said, 'What do you suppose that elephant is doing there?' The answer was: 'He is hatching an egg.' Then all I had to do was write a book about it. I've left that window open ever since, but it's never happened again."

Green Eggs and Ham
- Bennett Cerf, the founder and publisher of Random House, bet Seuss $50 that he couldn't write a book using just 50 words.
- Seuss won the bet. "It's the only book I ever wrote that still makes me laugh," he said 25 years later. He added: "Bennett never paid!"

Marvin K. Mooney, Will You Please Go Now?
"The puppylike creature constantly asked to 'go' is ex-President Richard M. Nixon."

The Lorax
Dr. Seuss's favorite book is, he said, "about people who raise hell in the environment and leave nothing behind." He wrote the story on a laundry list as he sat at a hotel pool in Kenya, watching a herd of elephants with his wife. "I wrote it as a piece of propaganda and disguised the fact," he told a reporter. "I wasn't afraid of preaching—but I was afraid of being dull."

Yertle the Turtle
"Yertle the turtle is Adolf Hitler."

The 500 Hats of Bartholomew Cubbins

In 1937 Seuss was on a commuter train in Connecticut. "There was a very stiff stockbroker sitting in front of me. I wondered what his reaction would be if I took his hat off and threw it out the window. I decided that he was so stuffy he would grow a new one."

The Cat in the Hat

• In 1954 *Life* magazine published excerpts of a report that analyzed how reading was taught in the Connecticut school system. In it, novelist John Hersey wrote that one of the major obstacles to learning was the dull material students were given—especially the illustrations. Kids, he said, should be inspired with "drawings like the wonderfully imaginative genius, Dr. Seuss."

• A textbook publisher read the article and agreed. He contacted Dr. Seuss and asked him to create a reading book. The publisher sent Seuss a list of 400 words he could use in the book. The reason: People felt this was the maximum that "kids could absorb at one time."

• "Geisel went through the list once, twice and got nowhere," reports *Parents* magazine. "He decided to give it one more shot; if he could find two words that rhymed, they'd form the title and theme of the book. Within moments, *cat* and *hat* leaped off the page. But then it took him nine months to write the entire book."

*   *   *

"Unless someone like you cares a whole awful lot,
Nothing is going to get better. It's not."

—**Dr. Seuss**

Before the 1920s, pink was considered a color for boys.

MORE GROSS STUFF

Essential (but nasty) information about your body.

TOE JAM

What exactly is that gray, dust bunny-looking stuff between your toes? Some people call it "toe jam," but—yuck!—you'd never even think about smearing it on a piece of toast!

So where does it come from? Most mornings you slip on a pair of socks and put your feet into a pair of shoes. As you walk around all day, your skin sheds dead cells. Some drift into the air or into your clothes. But the cells on your toes have no place to go, except into those nice little spaces between the toes. Take these dead cells and add some moisture from your feet—which are sweating inside those shoes and socks—and the combination creates a nice gray goo. Then add some fuzz and bits of thread from your socks.

Now, have you ever rolled a little ball of clay between your fingers? That's what your toes are doing with the dead cells, the moisture, and the fuzz. Toss in some of the dirt you picked up from walking around barefoot before you put on your socks, and you've got a little ball of toe jam.

If all the ice in Antarctica melted, the oceans would rise about 200 feet.

THE BIRTH OF THE BURGER

BRI member and food historian Jeff Cheek contributed this fascinating history of the hamburger.

WILD HORSEMEN

In the 13th century, wild nomadic horsemen known as Tartars overran most of Asia and eastern Europe. They had a distinct way of preparing meat: They sliced off a large chunk of horse meat or beef and slipped it under the saddle. A day of hard riding would tenderize it. Then it was chopped up and eaten raw.

This custom was introduced into the area we now call Germany by traders traveling down the Elbe River to Hamburg. The German people did not eat horse meat, but they did start serving ground raw beef flavored with garlic, spices, and a raw egg. (Today, it's called "steak tartare" and is still popular in Europe and North America.)

For those who preferred their beef cooked, those beef patties became the first hamburger steaks…but they weren't the handheld sandwiches we call hamburgers. Those were invented hundreds of years later.

DINNER IN HAMBURG

It all began around 1880, in a restaurant near the docks of the Hamburg-Amerika Line in Hamburg, Germany. Owner Otto Kuase began serving a sandwich American sailors loved: two slices of buttered bread, pickle strips, and a fried beef patty with a butter-fried egg on top. It made an excellent, inexpensive dinner.

So many Yankee seamen came to his restaurant for the sandwich that Kuase listed it on his menu as "American Steak." When the sailors returned home, they taught restaurants along the eastern seaboard how to make it. Soon, all a customer had to say was "bring me a Hamburger" (from the city of Hamburg). The name stuck even when the recipe changed.

THE BURGER STARTS SIZZLING

In 1904, to celebrate the centennial of the Louisiana Purchase, St. Louis staged a huge World's Fair. There were hundreds of vendors selling foods—including German immigrants peddling a new version of the hamburger. The slices of bread were replaced with dinner rolls, which fit the round meat patty. Butter was expensive, so the rolls were smeared with ketchup, which was cheaper. The butter-fried egg was replaced with slices of onion and tomato. The pickles remained.

The new hamburger was inexpensive because cheap cuts of beef could be used, and it was an instant success. People from all over the United States attended the fair and returned home ready to eat more hamburgers.

THE BUN

There was one flaw with the new design—the dinner rolls made the burgers harder to eat. So for another dozen years or so, people kept using the traditional slices of bread. Then an enterprising cook in Wichita, Kansas, invented the last component of the modern hamburger: he created a round, soft bun that absorbed the juices of the meat patty.

His name was J. Walter Anderson and he was working as a short-order cook when he made his invention. Soon after, he bought an old trolley and converted it into a five-stool diner specializing in burgers at 5¢ each. This was in 1916, but it was a real bargain even then. In 1920 Anderson added two more diners, stressing their cleanliness with the name White Castle Hamburgers. Other restaurants followed, and White Castle soon became the first national hamburger chain.

* * *

WHAT'S IN A NAME

At the beginning of World War I, the emperor of Germany, Kaiser Wilhelm, had a treaty with Belgium guaranteeing its neutrality. When he sent his armies through Belgium to attack France, the U.S. protested— and the Kaiser replied that the treaty was just "a scrap of paper." It was a public relations disaster—anti-German hysteria swept the world. On American menus, sauerkraut became "victory cabbage" and hamburger steak became Salisbury Steak. But against pressure to call burgers "ground meat patty sandwiches," burger-lovers held their ground. Today, a hamburger is still a hamburger.

Two things U.S. kids spend the most money on: 1. Food and drink, 2. Toys and games.

CARTOON NAMES

How did our favorite cartoon characters get their unusual names? Here are a few answers.

Casper the Friendly Ghost: Cartoonist Joe Oriolo's daughter was afraid of ghosts—so he invented one that wouldn't scare her. "We were looking for a name that didn't sound threatening."

Mickey Mouse: Walt Disney wanted to name the character Mortimer Mouse—but his wife hated the name. "Mother couldn't explain why the name grated; it just did," Disney's daughter Diane remembers. Disney wanted the character's name to begin with the letter M (to go with Mouse) and eventually decided on Mickey.

Porky Pig: According to creator Bob Clampett: "Someone thought of two puppies named Ham and Ex, and that started me thinking. So after dinner one night, I came up with Porky and Beans. I made a drawing of this fat little pig, which I named Porky, and a little black cat named Beans."

Rocky and Bullwinkle: Rocky was picked because it was "just a square-sounding kid's name"; Bullwinkle was named after Clarence Bulwinkel, a used-car dealer from Berkeley, California.

Elmer Fudd: Inspired by a line in a 1920s song called "Mississippi Mud." The line: "It's a treat to meet you on the Mississippi Mud—Uncle Fudd."

Michael Jackson was awarded his first gold record when he was 11 years old.

WEATHER REPORT

A few random facts about the weather.

IS FOG JUST A CLOUD?

More or less. Fog and clouds are both made up of tiny droplets of water. Clouds form high in the sky and fog forms near the ground, but the process that creates them is the same. Most fog happens when moist warm air collides with cold ground. The moisture condenses into tiny droplets which form a cloud…of fog. It takes trillions of these tiny drops to make one teaspoon of water!

RAIN FACTS

- At the center of most raindrops is a tiny speck of dust.
- Raindrops are actually round, not tear-shaped.
- Heavy rain falls at about 30 feet per second. But drizzle can take an hour to hit the ground.
- Meghalaya, India, is one of the wettest places on Earth, with 467 inches of rain per year.
- It didn't rain in Calama, Chile, from 1570 to 1971—that's 400 years!

OVER THE RAINBOW

After it rains, the air is full of tiny drops of water. When sunlight passes through those drops of water, they act like prisms and split the light into the colors of the spectrum—red, orange, yellow, green, blue, indigo, and violet—making a rainbow.

An estimated 16 million tons of rain fall to Earth every second.

MYTH AMERICA

Here are two stories that we now recognize as American myths…but they were taught as historical facts for many years. These might surprise you.

MANHATTAN ISLAND
The Myth: In 1626 Peter Minuit bought Manhattan Island from the Canarsee Indians for $24 worth of beads and other trinkets.

The Truth: Minuit *did* trade 60 guilders (roughly $24) worth of beads, knives, axes, clothes, and rum to Chief Seyseys of the Canarsee tribe "to let us live amongst them" on Manhattan Island—but the Canarsee actually got the best of the deal…because they didn't own the island in the first place. They lived on the other side of the East River, in what is now Brooklyn, and only visited the southern tip of Manhattan to fish and hunt.

The Weckquaesgeeks tribe, which lived on the upper three-fourths of the island, had a much stronger claim to it, and were furious when they learned they'd been left out of the deal. They fought with the Dutch settlers for years until the Dutch finally paid them, too.

THE LIBERTY BELL
The Myth: The Liberty Bell, which rang at the first public reading of the Declaration of Independence, has

---

You were born without kneecaps. (So was everybody else.)

always been a precious symbol of our nation's heritage.

The Truth: The bell, which was installed in the Pennsylvania State House in Philadelphia in 1753, was almost sold off as scrap metal in 1828.

According to one account, the building was being refurbished and the Philadelphia city fathers wanted a new bell. So they hired a bell maker from Germantown, Pennsylvania, named John Wilbank to make a replacement for the Liberty Bell and even got him to agree to take the old bell away. But when Wilbank went to collect the 2,000-pound relic, he changed his mind. Why? It wasn't worth the trouble—the scrap value of the bell was less than what it would cost him to haul it away.

The city of Philadelphia actually sued to force him to take it. But Wilbank just gave it back to them as a gift, unaware that he'd just given away what would become one of the most respected symbols of freedom and independence in American history.

Q: What was Little Red Riding Hood's first name?   A: Blanchette.

LOONEY LAWS

Believe it or not, these laws are real!

It's illegal to ride an ugly horse down the street in Wilbur, Washington.

It's against the law to step out of an airplane while it's in the air over Maine.

Ninth-grade boys can't grow mustaches in Binghamton, New York.

It's against the law to drink milk on a train passing through North Carolina.

You can't carry an ice cream cone in your pocket in Lexington, Kentucky.

It's illegal to spit against the wind in Sault Sainte Marie, Michigan.

Goats can't legally wear trousers in Massachusetts.

In Lawrence, Kansas, it's against the law to carry bees around in your hat on city streets.

Oregon prohibits citizens from wiping their dishes. You must let them drip-dry.

It's illegal to swim on dry land in Santa Ana, Ca.

If you mispronounce "Arkansas" when you're in that state, you're breaking the law.

It's illegal to play cards in the road in Somerset County, Maryland.

You can't go barefoot in Austin, Texas, without a $5 permit.

In Hartford, Connecticut, it's illegal to educate your dog.

Salt is the only rock humans can eat.

FIGHTING FIRE WITH FIRE

When we look for ways to preserve our natural environment, our best teacher may be...Mother Nature.

O N TOP OF OLD SMOKEY
Here's an idea that may shake you up: Forest fires can be a good thing. Does this mean that Smokey Bear is wrong?

Not exactly. Smokey's right about preventing fires caused by human carelessness—but the truth is, fire is a natural process and part of a forest's life cycle. And if we don't do carefully planned and safely executed "prescribed burns," we may actually speed up the decline of our public lands.

PUT OUT THE FIRE

More than 100 years ago, people began putting out forest fires, whether of natural or human origin, as soon as possible, to protect themselves and their property. But putting out every wildfire allowed some forests to grow too many trees, well beyond the capacity of the available land and water to sustain them.

NATURE'S REMEDY

As a doctor prescribes medicine for sick people, forest

managers now prescribe fire for unhealthy forests over-populated with weak and diseased trees. This approach is actually a return to the historical and natural role of fire: to clean out weakened vegetation, reduce disease and pests—and make room for new plants.

But won't this new approach possibly destroy entire forests, and threaten houses and recreation areas? On the contrary, a carefully planned and controlled fire gets rid of natural "fuels" such as brush, dead trees, fallen leaves, and trees that are growing too closely together. Later, if there *is* a fire started by lightning or human carelessness, there's less danger of it becoming a catastrophe.

DANGER ZONE

Are "prescribed" fires totally without dangers? Critics of the system point to the damage caused by the Yellowstone National Park fires of 1988.

Here's what happened: When lightning-caused fires began on July 14, park officials decided to let them run their natural course, as nature's way of renewing a wild area. But that summer was unusually dry—there was little rain to slow or extinguish the blaze. At the end of July, park officials still believed that rain was on its way…but they were wrong.

Instead of rain, they got the most powerful winds ever recorded in the month of August. By the time of the first extended rainstorm on September 11, the fires were blazing out of control.

More than 1.6 million acres burned in Yellowstone and surrounding forests that summer. Ten thousand firefighters battled blazes at a cost of more than $120 million. It wasn't until the first heavy snow covered the park in November that the fires finally went out.

A NEW POLICY

After the Yellowstone fires, there were many investigations. One report concluded that the "let it burn" policy had to be used on a case-by-case basis. Another advised that forest managers take precautionary steps to reduce the amount of natural fuel—in case of fire. And that brought about the practice of "prescribed" fires to thin forests of excess underbrush and trees.

Bonus: After being cleared by a prescribed fire, a forest begins to replenish itself. Areas cleared by fire become meadows, attracting wildlife. Soon these areas sprout species of trees that follow fire, such as fast-growing aspen. Later, other trees join in, and a new forest is created.

So, to maintain the health of a forest, sometimes fire can be considered as essential as water.

*　　*　　*

CREEPY CRAWLY NAME GAME

Q: How did the tarantula get its name?

A: From the Italian seaport city of Taranto, where the hairy spider comes from.

Proper English: Technically speaking, a female "dude" is known as a "dudine."

BATHROOM LORE

*More history of the room you
might be sitting in right now.*

T HE MODERN FLUSH TOILET
• The modern flush toilet was invented by
Englishman Alexander Cumming in 1775.

• Cumming's toilet emptied directly into a pipe,
which then carried the waste to a cesspool.

• Other toilets had done this, but Cumming's
improvement was the "stink trap" that kept water
in the pipe and thus blocked odor.

• It is widely believed that an Englishman
named Thomas Crapper invented the toilet—
but that's a myth.

HEAD FOR THE JOHN

• In the mid-1500s in England, a chamber pot
was referred to as a "jake." A hundred years
later, it became a "john," or "cousin john." In the
mid-1800s, it was also called a "joe."

• That still may not be the source of the term *john* for
the bathroom. In the 1920s, men's and women's rest-
rooms became common in public places. They were
sometimes referred to as "johns" and "janes."

• The term *potty* comes from the pint-sized chamber
pots built for kids.

BODY MUSIC: THE FART

*Here's more about that fine musical instrument: your body.
Feel free to play along as you read about...the fart.*

LET 'ER RIP!
There are few things more embarrassing than
hearing an accidental trumpet blast explode out
of your south end.

There are many names for this sound: fart, flatus,
flatulence, passing gas, breaking wind, morning thunder, etc. Some witty folks refer to farts as "barking spiders" or "low-flying ducks." And there are several types:
the loud, boisterous kind...the bubbling, gurgling
kind...the high-pitched squeaker...and the dreaded
SBD—silent, but deadly.

WHO CUT THE CHEESE?
Whatever you call it, a fart is just a lot of gas. Nitrogen, carbon dioxide, oxygen, methane, and hydrogen
sulfide, to be exact. When you eat foods that your
stomach can't digest or if you swallow too much air,
gas builds up in your stomach. That gas has got to go
somewhere and the only places it can go is either out
through your mouth or out the other end.

So why do farts smell? The culprit is hydrogen sulfide gas. This gas contains sulfur, which causes farts to

have a smelly odor like a rotten egg. The more sulfur you have in your diet, the more your farts will stink. The smelly offenders are beans (of course!), eggs, onions, broccoli, Brussels sprouts, cabbage, and cauliflower.

BEANS, BEANS, THE MUSICAL FRUIT, THE MORE YOU EAT, THE MORE YOU TOOT!

You probably know that eating beans makes you fart...but why? Beans contain a type of sugar called *raffinose* that your body can't use. Cabbage, broccoli, Brussels sprouts, and cauliflower are loaded with raffinose, too. So are whole grains. And speaking of sugar, *sorbitol* (which is found in pears, apples, and sugar-free chewing gum), has been the cause of many a stinky squeaker.

Drinking carbonated drinks can cause a gassy build-up because of another kind of sugar—*fructose*. Of course, the carbonated bubbles will give you a double-whammy blast of air into your belly.

Milk and cheese contain yet another kind of sugar—*lactose*, which can be a real problem for people who are "lactose intolerant." This means their bodies can't process milk or cheese so their intestines must work extra hard to move that food through their bodies. And these culprits don't go quietly.

SHOT HEARD 'ROUND THE WORLD

Why do some farts sneak out in a quiet way and some break the sound barrier? It all has to do with the trip from the stomach to the other end. Have you ever

Donald Duck's middle name is Fauntleroy.

wrung out a towel? You squeeze one section at a time, moving your hands down the length of the towel until all of the water runs out. That's the way your intestines move food and gas. If certain foods are hard to digest, then they'll have a rougher ride because your intestines have to work hard and fast to propel them through your body. That makes the food—and gas—travel faster and faster, and the gas explodes out of your rear end. Food that's easier to digest travels at a nice slow pace and the gas simply "whiffs" out.

PUT A CORK IN IT

So how do you keep from being voted Most Likely to Let One Fly?

• Don't gulp your food. When you chow down, take time to chew. Eating too fast makes you swallow air, which then builds up in your stomach. The resulting gassy build-up can clear a room.

• Exercise. If you keep your outsides fit, your insides will be fit, too. Exercise not only prevents flatulence but it also helps get rid of that bloated feeling. A nice brisk walk in the fresh air will do wonders for your digestive system.

WORDS OF WISDOM

Benjamin Franklin said, "Fart proudly." Uncle John says, "If someone stretches out their hand to you and begs you to pull their finger—don't do it!"

Each year, 16,000 cheerleaders seek emergency room treatment for cheer-related injuries.

REEL WISDOM

Some wise words from the movies.

"Try not. Do…or do not—there is no try."
—Yoda, *The Empire Strikes Back*

"There seems to be no sign of intelligent life anywhere."
—Buzz Lightyear, *Toy Story*

"There is a difference between knowing the path and walking the path."
—Morpheus, *The Matrix*

"Life moves pretty fast. If you don't stop and look around once in a while you could miss it."
—Ferris Bueller, *Ferris Bueller's Day Off*

"The wise speak only of what they know."
—Gandalf, *The Lord of the Rings*

"As a matter of cosmic history, it has always been easier to destroy than to create."
—Mr. Spock, *Star Trek II*

"Stupid is as stupid does."
—*Forrest Gump*

"When you're the middle child in a family of five million, you don't get any attention."
—Z, *Antz*

"Man who catch fly with chopsticks can accomplish anything."
—Mr. Miyagi, *The Karate Kid*

"You see, flying takes three things: hard work, perseverance and…hard work."
—Rocky Rhodes, *Chicken Run*

Film fact: Clint Eastwood was the #1 box office star in both the 1970s and the 1980s.

COLORS

Colors have a lot more impact on our daily lives than you might think. Here are some things researchers have found out about people and color.

BLUE

• Blue has a tranquilizing effect. Bridges are often painted blue to discourage suicide attempts. And according to one report: "When schoolroom walls were changed from orange to blue, students' behavior and learning comprehension soared."

GREEN

• Because it reminds us of fields and foliage, green makes us feel secure. Researchers say it's a good color for bedrooms and kitchens.

• Studies show that people working in green environments get fewer stomach aches than they do in areas where other colors predominate.

YELLOW

• It's the color most likely to stop traffic.

• But yellow also represents "caution or temporariness—so car rental agencies and taxis use it, but not banks."

• Too much yellow makes people anxious. "Babies cry more and people lose their tempers more in yellow rooms."

RED

• Red is a stimulant. It can cause insomnia if it's used in bedrooms.

• Studies show red makes people oblivious to how much time is passing. That's why it's used in bars and casinos—they want you to stay longer and spend more money.

ASK THE EXPERTS

*More cosmic questions, with answers
from America's trivia experts.*

B
LINDED BY THE LIGHT

Q: *Why do moths fly into the light?*

A: "Moths aren't really attracted to light. Somehow the brightness confuses their sense of direction and they can't fly straight anymore. Scientists still don't completely understand why. But they do know that, unlike human beings, moths use light rays from the moon or sun as a guide when they fly. The moth keeps itself moving in a straight line by constantly checking its position against the angle of the light rays striking its eyes.

"Although this complicated guidance system works fine when the light source is far away, it goes haywire when the light is close by. Stimulated by a bulb or candle, the moth's nervous system directs its body to fly so that both eyes receive the same amount of light. This locks the helpless creature onto a course toward the light and eventually causes it to blunder right into the bulb or flame." (From *How Do Ants Know When You're Having a Picnic?*, by Joanne Settel and Nancy Baggett)

LIKE A FISH UNDERWATER

Q: *Can a fish drown?*

A: Believe it or not, yes. "Fish, like people, need oxygen to live. There is oxygen both in the air and in the water. People breathe in the oxygen of the air through their lungs. When a person drowns, it's because they have used up their supply of oxygen and cannot get any from the water. So they die. Fish breathe through gills rather than lungs. Gills can extract oxygen from water, but not from air. When a fish is pulled out of water, it soon exhausts its supply of oxygen, and 'drowns' because its gills can no longer function." (From *A Book of Curiosities*, by Roberta Kramer)

AFTER-DINNER DIP?

Q: *Should you really wait an hour after eating before going swimming?*

A: "Water safety experts used to think that stomach cramps caused by swimming on a full stomach were a cause of drowning. The cramps would cause you to double up in pain, you'd sink like a stone, and that would be the end of you. Later research, however, showed that stomach cramps were rare. It's still not wise to swim long distances on a full stomach because you might become dangerously tired. But splashing around in the pool is harmless." (From *Know It All*, by Ed Zotti)

Do you want to be a *herpetologist*? That's someone who studies reptiles and amphibians.

TOYS THAT FLOPPED

Toys don't just magically appear—somebody thinks them up. And sometimes toy designers have no idea what will appeal to kids. Here are a few unbelievable goofs.

T**HUGGIES DOLLS**
Introduced in the summer of 1993, Thuggies came with something that no dolls had ever had before—criminal records. There were 17 different characters, with names like "Motorcycle Meany," "Bonnie Ann Bribe," and "Mikey Milk 'em."

The dolls were designed to discourage crime. Each one came packaged in a prison cell and had its own rehabilitation program. Children were supposed to set them on the straight-and-narrow. (Bonnie Ann Bribe, for example, had to read to senior citizens an hour a day.) The dolls even came with a gold star to wear when they successfully completed their rehabilitation.

MARYBEL GET WELL DOLL
Ever pretend to be sick? Then maybe Marybel Get Well is for you. This hypochondriac doll from Madame Alexander came with crutches, a cast for her leg, bandages, pills, quarantine signs, and measles spots.

FLUBBER
Hasbro's Flubber was tied to Walt Disney's 1962 hit film, *Son of Flubber*. "Flubber acts amazing," the compa-

---

Fast asleep: An albatross seabird can fly as fast as 25 mph while sleeping.

ny proclaimed. "It bounces so high. It floats like a boat. It flows and moves." Flubber was made out of synthetic rubber and mineral oil, so it was cheap to produce…but it had one problem—it made people sick.

More than 1,600 parents and kids came down with sore throats, rashes, and other reactions from handling the stuff. Hasbro had to recall Flubber…and then find a way to get rid of it. It floated, so they couldn't dump it in the ocean; they couldn't burn it, because it gave off "noxious black smoke"…so they buried it and then put a parking lot over it. (According to company legend, "on hot summer days, Flubber oozed through cracks in the pavement.") Hasbro had been profitable in 1961, but Flubber almost put them out of business in 1963.

ANGEL BABIES

In the 1970s, the Ideal Toy Corp. had a product called Fairies. They were tiny dolls with mechanical fluttering wings, and might have sold quite well…if someone hadn't insisted on changing the name to "Angel Babies." They had to change the doll, too. "Now," says one toy industry insider, "they were these chunky little toddlers with halos and wings. They lived on clouds, played harps, very cute." Ideal introduced the toy at the annual New York Toy Fair and waited for Christmas orders to pour in. They never came.

Why? Ideal forgot something important: "Angel Babies" means they're dead babies. The idea of dead baby dolls was too creepy for parents to even consider buying for their kids.

MYTHICAL CREATURES

Everyone knows about dragons and unicorns. Here are the origins of some other legendary beasts from ancient mythology.

C**reature:** Centaur
Where It's From: Greece
Creature's Features: The *Centaur* has the body of a horse but the torso and head of a man. There are two types of Centaurs: One type has the reputation for being a hotheaded warrior, and represents the worst in human behavior. In fact, some legends say the Centaur is the Devil himself. The other type of Centaur is learned and studious. The most famous of this kind was Chiron, who tutored the greatest Greek warriors, including Jason, Hercules, and Achilles.

Creature: Phoenix
Where It's From: Phoenicia (Lebanon)
Creature's Features: The *Phoenix* is a legendary bird with a special gift. Every thousand years, it flies to Phoenicia (or Arabia, in some tales) and builds a nest in the tallest palm tree it can find. Then it sets itself on fire. That may sound like a bad idea, except that nine days later, a new Phoenix rises from the ashes and flies off to live for another millennium. If you hear

---

Wide open spaces: Fewer people live in Wyoming than live in any other state (494,423).

someone say, "He rose like a Phoenix," or "like a Phoenix rising"—they're usually describing someone who has had a disaster in his life but was able to "rise above it" and start anew.

Creature: Satyr
Where It's From: Greece
Creature's Features: The *Satyr* is often called a goat-man. That's because this creature is a man from the waist up but has the legs, hooves, and tail of a goat. He also has pointed ears and horns coming out of his forehead. The Satyr is the original party animal, especially when there's good food and wine to be had. Satyrs stay deep in the woods, chasing pretty young nymphs, playing their flutes, and dancing. Pan, the Greek god of nature and son of the god Hermes, was the most famous Satyr. He spent a lot of time playing his flute-like invention, the panpipes.

Creature: Basilisk
Where It's From: Cyrenaica (Libya)
Creature's Features: Legend says the *Basilisk* has the head and body of a rooster and the tail of a scorpion. But nobody would know for sure, since there's no way to see one and live to tell about it—just looking at a Basilisk will kill you. This small but mighty beast hisses like a snake and spits rocks. Plants die under its feet; birds die while flying over it. The Basilisk is found only in the desert. That's because it turns every land it passes through into a wasteland.

Would you like to be an *entomologist*? That's someone who studies bugs.

EMOTICONS

Ever wonder about those little faces that you see in e-mails? They're called "emoticons." Here are some of our favorites.

Emoticon	What It Means
:)	"Just kidding."
;)	"Wink wink"
:D	"I'm laughing!"
:-o	"Oh, noooo!"
:-(	"That makes me sad."
:-P	"I'm sticking my tongue out.'
:-#	"Don't tell anyone."
:-$	"Put your $ where your mouth is."
!-(	"I have a black eye."
:-*	"Here's a kiss."
I-(	"I'm sleepy."
:^)	"I've got a big nose."
:*)	"Just clowning around."
:-{#}	"I have braces."
O:-)	"I'm an angel."
:-IK-	"This is a formal message."
d:-)	"Look at my baseball cap."
@>--->----	"A rose just for you."
:-S	"I'm confused."

THE CASE OF THE MISSING BODY PARTS

This chapter was inspired by an article Uncle John read about the fact that Albert Einstein's brain was removed when he died. He wondered if other famous people "lost" a body part or two when they died. So he did some research…and was surprised by what he found.

WHERE IS EINSTEIN'S BRAIN?

Location: Lawrence, Kansas

How It Got There: When Einstein died in April 1955, he left a request that his friend and colleague Dr. Harry Zimmerman examine his brain. So Dr. Thomas Harvey, the pathologist who performed the autopsy on Einstein, removed the brain and had it cut into 200 pieces, some of which he gave to Zimmerman. The rest (representing about 75% of Einstein's brain) he took home and stored in formaldehyde-filled jars that he kept under his sink for nearly 40 years—occasionally giving out specimens to research scientists. (One such researcher keeps his section in his refrigerator, in a jar labeled "Big Al's Brain.")

At last report, Harvey, who had lost his medical license and was working in a plastics factory, was look-

---

The Italian astronomer Galileo went blind studying the sun through telescopes.

ing for a research lab or museum to take the rest of Einstein's brain and preserve it as an historical artifact.

WHERE ARE SAINT NICK'S FINGERS?

Location: Now on display in the city of Antalya, Turkey

How They Got There: Saint Nicholas, the Catholic bishop believed to be the inspiration for Santa Claus, died in the fourth century A.D. He was buried in his old church in the Turkish town of Demre. But somehow, his remains ended up in a church in the Italian city of Bari (tradition has it that Italian merchants from Bari stole them in 1087). The town of Demre has been trying to get the bones back for 900 years. All they have left is "a finger or two."

"One reason Christians aren't keen to send the bones back," the *Wall Street Journal* reports, "is because Turkey is now predominantly Moslem. In fact, some believe the 11th-century Christian monks in Myra allowed the Italians to remove the bones in order to save them from the advancing Turkish armies."

Muammer Karabulut, chairman of the Santa Claus Foundation, says his group's mostly Moslem membership should not be an issue. After all, he insists, "Santa Claus is [a] universal figure."

WHERE IS STONEWALL JACKSON'S ARM?

Location: The Civil War battle site at Chancellorsville, near Fredericksburg, Virginia

How It Got There: On May 2, 1863, as he was return-ing to camp after an important victory for the Confed-eracy, the legendary general was accidentally shot by his own troops. Jackson was hit in the left wrist and shoul-der, and his left arm had to be amputated.

Confederate troops buried the arm in a nearby field, complete with a religious ceremony and a marble tomb-stone. When Jackson died from complications eight days later, he was buried in Lexington, Virginia.

In 1929 the arm was dug up and reburied in a steel box on a nearby plantation. Near the field in which it now lies, there is a single gravestone marking the remains of Jackson's arm.

*   *   *

ASK THE EXPERTS

Q: *How does a magician pull a rabbit out of a hat?*
A: "The magician's table is draped with a cloth to pre-vent the audience from seeing a small shelf at the back of the table, upon which the bunny sits, wrapped in a large handkerchief. At the outset of the trick, the magi-cian removes his hat and displays the inside—empty. Then he sets it, brim down, near the back of the table. While waving his wand with his right hand, he grasps both the brim of the hat and the corners of the handker-chief with his left. With a swift, graceful—and unseen—move, he turns over the hat. The bundle drops into the hat and with another wave of his wand—presto, he raises the rabbit into the air." (From *More How Do They Do That?*, by Caroline Sutton and Kevin Markey)

Male patients fall out of hospital beds twice as often as female patients do.

BEWARE: HAUNTED HOUSE

A few more stories of ghosts and things that go bump in the night. BOO!

HAUNTED HOUSE: The Alamo, Texas
GHOST STORY: Remember the Alamo? That's the mission fort in San Antonio where a few hundred Texans led by Davy Crockett and Jim Bowie held off 4,000 Mexican soldiers for 11 days in 1836. The Texans refused to surrender and most were killed in the battle. The Mexican general Santa Ana ordered the fort to be torn down. But when his soldiers tried to break down the walls, "ghostly hands" reached out to stop them. The soldiers ran away in fear, and the fort still stands today. Visitors who stay in a nearby hotel report seeing horrible apparitions late at night coming out of the fort's walls. And many others have seen a ghost on top of the parapet, walking back and forth, trying to find a way to escape.

HAUNTED HOUSE: Rose Hall Plantation, Jamaica
GHOST STORY: Annie Palmer was the cruel owner of the plantation and was murdered by her slaves. It seems that now Annie's ghost likes to have her picture taken. Numerous visitors have reported finding strange images in their pictures when they get them developed.

According to market research, if a girl owns one Barbie, she probably owns seven.

Some see a woman's face in the mirror in Annie's bedroom. Others see a glowing spot above her bed. This ghost is also picky about who gets to take pictures in her house. Sometimes people find that any pictures they took inside the house have a misty look to them or don't come out at all—yet their outside pictures are fine. Don't believe it? Go to Rose Hall. You'll find many of these mystery pictures on display in the gift shop.

HAUNTED HOUSE: *Queen Mary* ocean liner
GHOST STORY: During the 1920s and 1930s, whenever the rich and famous wanted to cross the Atlantic, they rode the *Queen Mary*. She was the most glamorous ocean liner of her day. Today she's a floating hotel, permanently docked in Long Beach, California, but her ghosts sail on. If you want to meet a few, start with Door 13 in the engine room. It's haunted by the ghost of a young sailor who was crushed trying to escape a fire. People have heard knocking, seen smoke, and even felt the heat from the fire.

Drop by the check-in desk of the boat's hotel. You might see a lady in white, who walks behind a pillar and never appears on the other side. Or you may catch a glimpse of a ghostly couple strolling arm in arm down the hall to their stateroom.

And be sure to visit the swimming pool. It's a good place to find a few kid ghosts. One is a little girl who used to slide down banisters and run all over the ship. Now she calls for her mother or roams the hall by the third floor nursery, looking for her doll.

25% of Americans believe in ghosts; 10% say they've seen one.

UNCLE JOHN'S TRI-CKY TRI-CKS

Ready for a challenge? Have fun with these triangle puzzles.

1. You Tri My Patience. This is an *equilateral* triangle, which means that all three sides are the same length. Now try these two puzzles:

a) Create two smaller *equilateral* triangles by moving just four matchsticks.

b) Create four even smaller *equilateral* triangles by moving just six matchsticks.

2. Tri, Tri Again. Try to turn the pyramid of 10 circles upside down, moving 1 circle at a time to a new position in which it touches 2 or more circles.

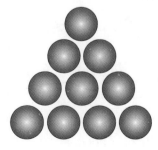

It's easy to do this in six moves. Can you do it in three?

Answers on page 281.

First country to allow women to vote: New Zealand, in 1893.

STRANGE TOURIST ATTRACTIONS

*The next time your parents want you to go to
a museum for an educational experience,
give them this list from Uncle John.*

THE POTATO MUSEUM

Location: Washington, D.C.

Background: Tom and Meredith Hughes have turned their love of the potato into a shrine to the noble tuber. This collection, located in their basement, proves that there is more to a spud than French fries. The museum has potato comic books, Mr. Potato Heads, potato cigarettes (*ugh*), potato chip cans, potato sacks, dead potato bugs, potato artwork, potato cookbooks, and a library of potato-themed books. Did you know that the world produces 300 million tons of potatoes a year? (Which country produces the most? Russia—they grow 25%.)

PAPER HOUSE MUSEUM

Location: Pigeon Cove, Massachusetts

Background: It took 20 years and 100,000 newspapers for the Stenman family to build this tiny house. It's only one room, but everything is made entirely of newspapers. The walls are made of 215 layers of newspaper. Fireplace, chairs, tables, desk—you guessed it—all out of newspaper.

Flush away! The average toilet will last about 50 years before it has to be replaced.

TATTOO ART MUSEUM

Location: San Francisco, California

Background: This museum is housed in a working tattoo parlor. Learn about the history of the tattoo in different societies, such as Japanese, Samoan, and Native American. But be forewarned: the owner, Lyle Tuttle, might be working on someone's body when you enter. And his collection of skin-engraving paraphernalia might make you think twice about that cute little butterfly you were thinking about putting on your ankle.

MUSEUM OF BATHROOM TISSUE

Location: Madison, Wisconsin

Background: This collection, housed in curator Carol Kolb's living room, includes hundreds of rolls of toilet paper from all over the United States and Europe. Look for rolls from the Statue of Liberty, the Metropolitan Museum of Art, and even Graceland, to name just three of the more than 3,000 samples. Kolb's friends are asked to bring back souvenir rolls from their trips abroad. Contributions welcomed.

METEOR CRATER MUSEUM

Location: Flagstaff, Arizona

Background: OK, so it's just a big hole in the ground, but the impact from a large meteor made the surrounding area look like the surface of the moon. NASA thought so too, and used the crater to train the *Apollo* astronauts.

MUSEUM OF BEVERAGE CONTAINERS

Location: Goodlettsville, Tennessee

Background: It all started in 1973, when Tom Bates started to pick up empty cans on the walk home from school. Now he has a museum and it's listed in the *Guinness Book of World Records* for its collection of 36,000 cans and bottles. Among the treasures: soft drinks with names like Zing, Zippy, and Zitz, a can of soda for pets, and camouflage cans produced for the U.S. Army during WWII.

NATIONAL PLASTICS CENTER AND MUSEUM

Location: Leominster, Massachusetts

Background: It's worth the trip just to see the Plastics Hall of Fame. Homage is paid to some of the greats, such as the inventors of Tupperware, Saran Wrap, and the Styrofoam cup. Important fact: Leominster is the birthplace of that fabulous tropical lawn ornament, the pink flamingo.

...AND HERE ARE A FEW MORE:

- **Hamburger Hall of Fame,** Seymour, WI

- **International Banana Museum,** Altadena, CA

- **Cockroach Hall of Fame,** Plano, TX

- **The Children's Garbage Museum,** Stratford, CT

- **Barney Smith Toilet Seat Art Museum,** San Antonio, TX.

A WEIRD FASHION QUIZ

Did you know that humans are the only animals who adorn their bodies simply for decoration? Think about it: did you ever see a squirrel wearing a necklace or a rabbit with a tatoo? Take this quiz and discover a few more strange fashion facts.

1. It was introduced in 1946, banned by beauty pageants, and named after a bombing target. What is it?

a) The girdle

b) The mini-skirt

c) The bikini

2. Who said: "I can't wear a pink shirt to work. Everybody wears white shirts. I'm not popular enough to be different."

a) President George W. Bush

b) Homer Simpson

c) David Letterman

3. In 1990 what modification was made to denim jeans in an attempt to increase sales?

a) Cuffs were added

b) They were dipped in beer

c) They were blasted full of holes with a shotgun

Star Trek's Captain Jean-Luc Picard's fish was named Livingston.

4. Bat guano (another name for…poop) used to be a key ingredient in what products?

a) Eyeliner and mascara

b) Halloween costumes

c) Glow-in-the-dark jewelry

5. The introduction of what household items in the early 1900s moved the focus of female beauty from the face to the entire body?

a) The full-length mirror and the bathroom scale

b) The television and the Polaroid camera

c) Talcum powder and deodorant

6. From 1000–500 B.C., warrior tribes from the western part of Europe did what to frighten their enemies?

a) Wore huge wigs so they looked twice as big

b) Dyed their bodies blue and fought naked

c) Charged backward with their butts bared

7. If you lived in the 1700s, you might have worn a "plumper," which was:

a) A puffy shirt

b) Padded underwear to make your butt look bigger

c) A cork ball inside your cheek where you were missing teeth

Answers

1. c; 2. b; 3. c; 4. a; 5. a; 6. b; 7. c

Among the other "treasures" found in King Tut's tomb: several vials of pimple cream.

NATURE'S RECIPE FOR RAIN

Did you know that the water you drink has been on the Earth since the beginning of time? Each drop of water is used again and again. It becomes rain through a system called "the water cycle." Here's how it works:

STEP ONE: Evaporation
Take one puddle of water on the Earth's surface. Heat with the sun until the puddle *evaporates* and becomes an invisible gas that rises into the air.

STEP TWO: Condensation
The vapor cools as it rises until it *condenses* and becomes a drop of water again.

STEP THREE: Precipitation
Watch the droplet fall to Earth as *precipitation*. Repeat as necessary, using the same water to make rain over and over again.

To Make Snow: Use the same recipe, but instead of cooling the vapor, *freeze* it. The vapor will condense and freeze, forming little ice crystals.

Carrots originally came from Afghanistan.

GANDHI'S WISDOM

Born in India in 1869, Mohandas K. Gandhi spent his life advocating freedom. He never waivered in his belief in nonviolent protest and religious tolerance.

"To believe in something, and not to live it, is dishonest."

"It is easy enough to be friendly to one's friends. But to be friends to the one who regards himself as your enemy is the quintessence of true religion. The other is mere business."

"An eye for an eye makes the whole world blind."

"For the nonviolent person, the whole world is one family. He will thus fear none, nor will others fear him."

"The earth provides enough to satisfy every man's needs, but not every man's greed."

"The only devils in the world are those running around in our own hearts— that is where the battle should be fought."

"I see neither bravery nor sacrifice in destroying life or property, for offense or defense."

"Retaliation is counter-poison and poison breeds more poison. The nectar of love alone can destroy the poison of hate."

"No culture can live if it attempts to be exclusive."

"Poverty is the worst form of violence."

"We must become the change we want to see in the world."

BIG, BAD BARBIE

*She's the world's favorite doll, a friend to millions of kids…
but don't mess with her—she'll sue the pants off you. How
scary can Barbie be? Just ask these former defendants.*

Lawsuit: *Barbie v. Barbara Bell*

Background: In 1992 Bell claimed she was
receiving psychic messages from Barbie. (Barbie's
first message: "I need respect.") For $3, she would chan-
nel Barbie's spirit and answer questions from Barbie fans.
She also published the *Barbie Channeling Newsletter*.

Here Comes Barbie: Mattel threatened a multimillion-
dollar lawsuit against Bell if she didn't shut down her
business and cease publication of her newsletter.

Outcome: Bell agreed…but she didn't see what all the
fuss was about. "Look, for $3 nobody's getting hurt," she
said, "and there are 700 million Barbie dolls in the
world with no voice."

Lawsuit: *Barbie v. Paul Hansen*

Background: Hansen sold "Barbie art" in the early
1990s. He changed normal Barbie dolls into weird characters like "Exorcist Barbie" and "Drag Queen Barbie."

Here Comes Barbie: When Mattel filed suit against
him, claiming $1.2 billion in damages, Hansen agreed
to sell his dolls only in art galleries…and to donate the
profits to charities. Good enough? Nope. Mattel wanted
to collect damages and win a stricter definition of "art

gallery." The judge ruled against Mattel "for not having a sense of humor."

Outcome: After a year of "heck," Hansen settled out of court and stopped making the dolls.

Lawsuit: *Barbie v. Paul David*

Background: David, a Barbie collector and publisher of a Barbie catalog, was in Mattel's good graces until the mid-1990s. Then he wrote in one of his catalogs that "if there were an ugly contest, Elizabethan Queen Barbie would win." He also forgot to put the registered trademark ® symbol on some Barbie photos.

Here Comes Barbie: Mattel swooped down and sued David for copyright infringement, accusing him of copying the company's packaging for his own use.

Outcome: David had to sign a settlement stipulating that Barbie would only be portrayed in his catalog as "wholesome, friendly, cheerful, kind, talented and fun-loving." Then in disgust he announced plans to sell his entire Barbie collection.

Lawsuit: *Barbie v. Mark Napier*

Background: Napier operated the Distorted Barbie website, which featured such "real-world Barbies" as "Fat and Ugly Barbie" and "Dolly Parton Barbie."

Here Comes Barbie: Mattel sent Napier a cease-and-desist letter telling him to shut down the site.

Outcome: Rather than do that, Napier just blurred the dolls' images…and replaced the "B" in Barbie with a "$".

First baseball game on TV: the Brooklyn Dodgers vs. the Cincinnati Reds, August 26, 1939.

CALCULATOR MAGIC

Got a calculator handy? If not, be sure to bring along one the next time you visit the "throne room," 'cause there's a lot more to numbers than just number one and number two.

NUMBER 7

Use a calculator to divide 1 by 7 (1 ÷ 7). Check out the answer. Now divide 2 and 3 and so on by 7 (2 ÷ 7, 3 ÷ 7, etc.). See what happens? The answer is always the numbers 142857 endlessly repeating. Seven is the only number that does this.

NUMBER 142,857

Here we are again. The number 142,857 is, well, stubborn. Multiply 142,857 by 2, then 3, then 4, or 5, or 6. What happens? The number just rearranges its figures, never giving them up. (But stop multiplying by the time you reach 7, because just like seventh grade, strange things start to happen.)

NUMBER 37

Pick a three-digit number in which all the digits are the same. For example, 333. Add the digits (3 + 3 + 3

Hi there. Enter the numbers 0.1134, then turn you calculator display upside down....

= 9). Divide the original number by the sum of its digits (333 ÷ 9). What's the answer? 37. Try some other numbers, like 111 ÷ 3, or 222 ÷ 6. The answer is always 37.

NUMBERS 11 AND 9091

Think of any five-digit number, like 15658 or 22222. Now multiply it by 11. Then multiply that number by 9091. And the answer is—your original five-digit number, twice! (Warning: Some calculators don't have enough slots for 10 digits, so you may need a fancier calculator or a computer to prove how weird these numbers are.)

NUMBERS 7 AND 11 AND 13

Pick a three-digit number from 100 to 999 and enter it twice into your calculator to produce a six-digit number. For example, 146,146. Now divide by 7, divide again by 11, and divide a third time by 13 (146,146 ÷ 7 = 20,878; 20,878 ÷ 11 = 1898; 1898 ÷ 13 = 146). Get it? The final answer is the same as your original three-digit number! A trio of weirdness!

NUMBER 9

Divide 1 by 9 (1 ÷ 9). Check out the answer. Now divide 2, 3, and so on by 9 (2 ÷ 9, 3 ÷ 9, etc.). You'll have to try it yourself to see the bizarre answers, but we will tell you this: 9 is the only number that makes this happen.

UNCLE JOHN: PUZZLE DETECTIVE

Ready for a challenge? Have fun with these puzzles.

Sitting Pretty. On a recent trip to Washington, D.C., Uncle John took time off from his busy schedule at the FBI to do a little sightseeing with his trusted assistant, J. Porter Newman. While gazing at the Lincoln Memorial, Uncle John suddenly blurted out, "Flying Flushes, Newman! Here's a puzzle! Name a place where your best friend can sit down…but you can't."

"I haven't a clue," said Newman.

"Dear boy," said Uncle John without taking his eyes off the statue of Abraham Lincoln. "Isn't it obvious?"

Handy Man. Uncle John and his trusted assistant, J. Porter Newman, were sitting in Uncle John's living room, each quietly reading a book, when Uncle John suddenly slammed his book shut and said, "Flying Flushes, Newman! Here's a puzzle! At our meeting of the Plunger Society last week, every person shook hands with every other person exactly once. If there were fifteen handshakes, how many people attended the meeting?"

"But that's impossible," said Newman.

"No, dear boy, it's elementary," said Uncle John.

How many people attended the meeting?

Answers on page 282.

In almost every language on Earth, the word for mother begins with the letter "m."

I TAWT I TAW A PUDDY TAT!

Sure, they're cartoon characters, but Tweety and Sylvester are still a classic comedy team—literally made for each other, right? Well, no. It actually took a few years before anyone thought of putting them in the same cartoon. Here's how it happened.

FIRST CAME TWEETY...

Created by: Looney Tunes director Bob Clampett

Inspiration: "In school I remember seeing nature films which showed newborn birds in a nest," Clampett recalled. "They always looked funny to me. One time I kicked around the idea of twin baby birds called 'Twick 'n' Tweet' who were precursors of Tweety."

• Tweety's basic design and "innocent stare at the camera" were copied from a nude baby picture of Clampett himself. That's probably why the original Tweety was pink.

Debut: "Tale of Two Kitties," a 1942 cartoon featuring two bumbling cats named Babbit and Cat-stello...and a nameless bird. The little bird's opening line, "I tawt I taw a puddy tat!" made the cartoon—and the character—a hit. The voice was supplied by Mel Blanc, who also did Daffy Duck, Bugs Bunny, and Porky Pig.

• Tweety's next cartoon, "Birdy and the Beast" (1944),

John Wilkes Booth's brother once saved the life of Abraham Lincoln's son.

gave him a name and a personality. But in 1946 censors said the pink bird "looked naked" and insisted Clampett put a pair of pants on him. The cartoonist refused; instead, he made Tweety yellow, with a slimmer body.

THEN CAME SYLVESTER...

Created by: Looney Tunes director Friz Freleng

Inspiration: Freleng designed the cat to look like a clown. "I gave him a big, red nose and a very low crotch, which was supposed to look like he was wearing baggy pants."

Debut: A 1945 cartoon called "Life with Feathers." The plot: "A love bird has a major fight with his wife and decides to end it all by letting a cat (Sylvester, before he had a name) eat him." The cat's first words, on finding a bird who wants to be eaten: "Thufferin' thuccotash!"

• Sylvester's voice—also supplied by Mel Blanc—sounded more like Blanc's real speaking voice than any of his other characters. Says Blanc in his autobiography, *That's Not All Folks*:

> When I was first shown Sylvester, with his floppy jowls and disheveled appearance, I said to Friz Freleng, 'A big sloppy cat should have a big shthloppy voice!' While recording Sylvester cartoons, my scripts would get so covered with saliva that I'd repeatedly have to wipe them clean. I used to suggest to actress June Foray, who played Tweety's vigilant owner, Granny, that she wear a raincoat to the [recording] sessions.

Tallest dog breed: The Irish Wolfhound, which can grow to 34 inches high at the shoulder.

TOGETHER AT LAST...

In 1947 Friz Freleng made the cartoon that paired the cat with Tweety. He gave the cat a name—Thomas (changed to Sylvester in 1948 by animator Tedd Pierce, who thought a slobbering cat needed a name that could be slobbered)—and made Tweety a little friendlier. "I made him look more like a charming baby, with a bigger head and blue eyes," Freleng explained.

In their first cartoon together, "Tweetie Pie," Thomas the cat catches Tweety, who's freezing in the winter cold. But before he can eat the bird, Thomas's owner saves it and brings it home. Tweety then proceeds to terrorize the cat and take over the house.

"Tweety Pie" earned the Warner Bros. cartoon studio its first Academy Award and started a partnership that lasted for dozens more cartoons, right up to 1996 when Tweety and Sylvester appeared together in the movie *Space Jam*.

*   *   *

RANDOM FACTS

• Kid power: In the United States, 40% of all purchases are made by or influenced by children.

• More than 12 million computers, amounting to more than 300 thousand tons of electronic garbage, are thrown away each year.

• In the Northern Hemisphere, most tornadoes twist counterclockwise. Below the equator, they spin the other way—clockwise.

HOW ALICE GOT TO WONDERLAND

When Charles Lutwidge Dodgson met four-year-old Alice Liddell in 1856, he wrote in his diary, "I mark this day with a white stone"—meaning that it was a wonderful day for him. It turned out to be a pretty good day for kids everywhere: Dodgson became famous as the author Lewis Carroll... and Alice Liddell was the child who inspired him to write Alice's Adventures in Wonderland.

BACKGROUND

Charles Lutwidge Dodgson was a deacon and professor of mathematics at Christ Church College in Oxford. In 1856, a new dean arrived—Henry George Liddell. Liddell had three children, and Dodgson quickly became friendly with them.

• The youngest, four-year-old Alice, had a special relationship with Reverend Dodgson—perhaps because her favorite expression was "Let's pretend."

DOWN THE RABBIT HOLE

On what he recalled as a "golden July afternoon" in 1862, Dodgson took the three Liddell girls—Alice, Lorina and Edith—boating on the river for a picnic.

• As they rowed lazily downstream, Alice begged Dodgson to tell them a story...so he made one up.

If you get three strikes in a row in bowling, it's called a *turkey.*

- He called his heroine Alice and began the story by sending her down a rabbit hole "without," he later explained, "the least idea what was to happen afterwards."

- Amazingly, he made up most of *Alice's Adventures in Wonderland* on the spot.

SAVING A TREASURE

Alice liked the story so much that she asked Dodgson to write it down. That very night, he wrote the whole thing out in longhand, adding his own illustrations. He called it *Alice's Adventures Underground*.

- Dodgson had already decided he needed a pen name for the poems and stories he'd been contributing to magazines. Why? He also wrote articles on mathematics and was afraid people wouldn't take him seriously if they knew he was writing nonsense rhymes.

- He scrambled the letters of his first two names, added a few more and came up with the name "Lewis Carroll," and used it when he signed *Alice's Adventures Underground* for Alice.

A BOOK IS BORN

But before Dodgson gave the handwritten manuscript to Alice, he happened to show it to a friend named George Mac-Donald, who read it to his children. The entire

MacDonald family loved the story so much that they urged Dodgson to publish it. If he hadn't shown it to them, Alice's adventures might have been nothing more than a personal gift to one little girl.

• After giving the original book to Alice Liddell as promised, Dodgson decided to take the MacDonalds' advice. He revised the story, added to it, and then hired John Tenniel, a well-known cartoonist, to illustrate it.

• The book was published in 1865 as *Alice's Adventures in Wonderland*. It became so popular that in 1872, Dodgson published the further adventures of Alice, entitled *Through the Looking Glass*.

FAMILIAR FACES

Many of the now-classic characters were easily recognizable to the Liddell children.

The White Rabbit was modeled after Dodgson himself—he was very proper, usually dressed in an old-fashioned formal black suit and top hat.

The Duck was Dodgson's friend, Robinson Duckworth.

The Lory and the Eaglet were Lorina and Edith Liddell.

And finally…the Dodo: The girls were fascinated by a stuffed dodo bird they'd seen in a museum. So Dodgson incorporated the bird into the story and modeled that one on himself, too. he stuttered—when he spoke his name, it came out as "Do-Do-Dodgson."

SPORTS SHORTS

Impress your friends with some of these little-known facts from the world of sports.

Clear Skating Ahead. Ice hockey is the only team sport that's divided into three time periods. Why? It used to be divided into halfs, but the ice got so rough and rutted during the game that they added an extra intermission...to clean off the playing surface.

Proud Papa. In the 1980s, Richard Williams made a bold prediction about his two baby girls: one day they would be the best tennis players in the world. When they grew up, Venus and Serena proved him right.

Not Enough Elbow Room. Lacrosse is a modern version of an ancient Native American game. Originally, teams sometimes had up to 1,000 players.

Rah Rah Rah! What do George W. Bush, Steve Martin, Ronald Reagan, Michael Douglas, and Aaron Spelling have in common? They were all former cheerleaders.

The Big Show. What TV show has the record for the most episodes ever? ESPN's SportsCenter. Since 1979, they've aired three shows a day, every day, totaling around 25,000 separate broadcasts by 2002.

Super Name. In 1967 Kansas City Chiefs owner Lamar Hunt saw his daughter bouncing a Superball, which gave him the inspiration for the name...Super Bowl.

Are you left-handed or right-handed? Either way, the nails on that hand grow the fastest.

THANKSGIVING MYTHS

It's one of American history's most familiar scenes: It's 1621. A small group of Pilgrims prepare a huge November feast to give thanks for a bountiful harvest and show their appreciation to the Native Americans who helped them survive their first winter. Together, they solemnly sit down to a meal of turkey, pumpkin pie, and cranberries. How accurate is this image of America's first Thanksgiving? Not very. Here are some common misconceptions about the origins of one of our favorite holidays.

MYTH: The settlers at the first Thanksgiving were called "Pilgrims."

TRUTH: They didn't refer to themselves as Pilgrims—they called themselves "Saints." Early Americans used the term *pilgrim* to refer to all early colonists. It wasn't until the 20th century that it was used exclusively to describe those who had landed on Plymouth Rock.

MYTH: The first feast took place in November.

TRUTH: It was actually sometime between late September and the middle of October—after the harvest had been brought in. By November, villagers were busy preparing for winter, salting and drying meat, and making their houses as wind-resistant as possible.

Benny Benson of Seward, Alaska, was only 13 when he designed the Alaska state flag.

MYTH: It was a solemn, religious occasion.

TRUTH: Hardly. It was a three-day harvest festival that included drinking, gambling, athletic games, and even target shooting with English muskets (which was intended as a friendly warning to the American Indians that the Pilgrims were prepared to defend themselves).

MYTH: They ate turkey.

TRUTH: Pilgrims ate deer, not turkey. Other foods they may have eaten: cod, bass, clams, oysters, Indian corn, native berries, water, beer, and an alcoholic drink the Pilgrims called "strong water."

One thing that definitely wasn't on the menu was pumpkin pie—in those days, the Pilgrims boiled their pumpkin and ate it plain.

MYTH: Pilgrims wore hats with buckles on them.

TRUTH: Pilgrims didn't dress in black, didn't wear buckles on their hats or shoes, and didn't wear tall hats. The 19th-century artists who painted them that way did so because they associated black clothing and buckles with being old-fashioned.

MYTH: Pilgrims held a similar feast every year.

TRUTH: There's no evidence that they celebrated again in 1622. The Pilgrims probably weren't in the mood—the harvest had been disappointing, and they were burdened with a new boatload of Pilgrims who had to be fed and housed through the winter.

How much is one decillion? That's a 1 with 33 zeroes after it.

YOU: THE ULTIMATE FOOD PROCESSOR

Get ready for a really gross journey through the human body.

DOWN THE HATCH

What do you get if you eat green grapes, white bread, yellow cheese, purple pudding, tan cereal, and pink cotton candy? Well, in a day or so, you'll get the same thing—brown poop. Where did all those colors go? Why does everything you eat turn brown?

Actually, the color is gone from something just a few minutes after you eat it. When food drops into your stomach, it's like it was dropping into a rubber bag and getting squirted with acid. Then the bag starts twisting and squeezing. Pretty soon, the acid and the squeezing not only destroy the food's color, but they also turn whatever you ate into a slimy liquid.

INTO A HOSE

OK, so your stomach is filled with slime that's full of acid. Now it's got to get rid of the acid. The slime drains out the bottom of your stomach into a tube that's kind of like a garden hose, called the *small intestine*. Here, it gets squirted with a liquid mixture of sodium bicarbonate. (Sodium bicarbonate is also called baking soda—the same stuff you see in the supermarket in those yellow boxes.)

How much is one centillion? That's a 1 with 303 zeroes after it.

The sodium bicarbonate neutralizes the acid and makes it harmless. But your body's not done yet. Other little hoses squirt chemicals that break the slime into molecules—really tiny little particles. Some of the chemicals also give the slime its color—greenish brown, kind of like pea soup.

HOW ABSORBING

Now the slimy green soup begins oozing through the small intestine, which is about an inch wide and 22 feet long.

The small intestine is designed to let molecules through its walls and into your bloodstream. It's during the trip through the small intestine that molecules of protein, carbohydrates, fat, vitamins, and minerals actually get into your body. It takes at least a few hours, and up to a day depending on what you eat.

...AND AWAY WE GO

When your body is done getting fed, what's left of the slime slides into a wider hose, called the *large intestine*. In an adult, the large intestine is nearly the size of a vacuum cleaner hose—about $2\frac{1}{2}$ inches wide and 5 feet long. In the large intestine, your body soaks up as many water molecules as it can get out of the slime. At the same time, waste products—old, dead blood cells and dead bacteria—are being dumped in. As the water leaves, the slime gets thicker, and the old, dead blood cells make the slime more brown. So, what's left is a thick brown paste.

Guess what happens next? That's right! And hey—be sure to flush when you're done.

Why are a woodpecker's nostrils covered with feathers? To keep out the sawdust.

COMPUTER FIRSTS

Some milestones from the Information Age.

1839: Two mathematicians, Charles Babbage and Ada Lovelace, invent the first true computer—a gear-driven mechanical calculator.

1945: ENIAC, the first electronic computer, is born. It is as big as a small house, weighs 30 tons, and is slower than a modern laptop.

1963: The first mouse is invented by engineer Doug Engelbart. It is made out of wood.

1964: IBM System 360 becomes the first computer to use removable disks (they are bigger than dinner plates). It also has the first keyboard.

1972: The first e-mail program is written by Ray Tomlinson. He is also the first to use the "@" symbol in an address.

1981: IBM introduces the personal computer.

1982: The Apple II+ becomes the first computer designed specifically for the classroom.

1989: Tim Berners-Lee coins the term *World Wide Web*.

1993: The year of the Internet—it starts with 600 websites and ends with more than 10,000.

1995: *Toy Story* is the first full-length computer-animated movie.

There were more than a billion websites in 2002.

FIREWORKS FACTS

Next July 4th, you'll have something new to talk about.

BACKGROUND
The first fireworks were hollowed-out bamboo stalks stuffed with black powder. The Chinese called them "arrows of flying fire" and shot them into the air during religious occasions and holidays to ward off imaginary dragons.

According to legend, the essential ingredient—black powder—was first discovered in a Chinese kitchen in the 10th century A.D. A cook was preparing potassium nitrate (a pickling agent and preservative) over a charcoal fire laced with sulfur. Somehow the three chemicals—potassium nitrate, charcoal, and sulfur—combined, causing an explosion. The meal was destroyed, but the powder, later known as gunpowder, was born.

SAFETY FIRST
According to fireworks industry estimates, as many people have been killed by Fourth of July fireworks as were killed in the Revolutionary War. Nearly all of the victims were killed setting off their own fireworks, not watching public displays. And most fatalities occurred before World War II, when fireworks were almost completely unregulated. The carnage was so widespread that the Fourth of July actually came to be known as the "Bloody Fourth," because of the large number of people

What's a *photic sneeze reflex*? Having to sneeze after you look at a bright light.

who were injured and who died from infected burns.

Then, in the 1930s, several organizations began a campaign to outlaw fireworks. Pressured by the *Ladies' Home Journal* (which printed gruesome photographs of maimed victims), the federal government and individual states started outlawing just about every kind of firework imaginable...to the point where many states now ban the sale of fireworks to the public entirely.

Since those days, the number of firework-related injuries has plummeted. Today, the Consumer Safety Commission ranks them as only the 132nd most-dangerous consumer item—behind such dangers as beds, grocery carts, key rings, and plumbing fixtures.

FIREWORKS COLORS

• Because black powder burns at a relatively low temperature, for more than 800 years fireworks burned only with dull yellow and orange flames. It wasn't until the 19th century that scientists discovered that mixing potassium chlorate into the powder made it burn much hotter, enabling it to turn different colors when different chemicals were added: For example, it burned red when strontium was added, green when barium was added, bright yellow when sodium was added, and white when aluminum, magnesium, and titanium were all added.

• Blues and violets (caused when copper and chlorine are added) are the hardest colors to create; even today, firework manufacturers' skills are judged according to how well their blues and violets turn out.

FIREWORKS LINGO

Here are some names the fireworks industry gives its creations:

- **Willows:** Fireworks with long colorful "branches" that stream down toward the ground.

- **Palm trees:** Willows that leave a brightly colored trail from the ground as they're shot into the air.

- **Chrysanthemums:** Fireworks that explode into perfect circles.

- **Split comets:** Fireworks that explode into starlets, which explode again into even more starlets.

- **Salutes:** A bright white flash followed by a boom.

- **Triple-break salutes:** Salutes that explode three times in rapid succession.

- **Cookie-cutters:** Created by filling the inside of a cardboard container with black powder and gluing individual starlets to the outside. When the black powder charge explodes, the starlets explode in the same shape as the cookie-cutter. Shapes include stars, hearts, ovals, and so on.

Ouch! Don Baylor was hit by a pitch 267 times in his career—a Major League record.

ANIMALS FAMOUS FOR 15 MINUTES

When 1960s pop artist Andy Warhol said, "In the future, everyone will be famous for 15 minutes," he probably didn't have animals in mind. Yet even they haven't been able to escape the publicity machine that keeps cranking out instant celebrities.

HEADLINE: *Cat Makes Weather Forecasters Look All Wet*

THE STAR: Napoleon, a cat in Baltimore

WHAT HAPPENED: In the summer of 1930, a severe drought hit Baltimore. Forecasters predicted an extended dry spell, but Frances Shields called local newspapers and insisted they'd have rain in 24 hours. The reason: Her cat was lying with his "front paw extended and head on the floor," and he only did that just before it rained. Reporters laughed...until there was a rainstorm the next day.

THE AFTERMATH: Newspapers across the country picked up the story, and Napoleon became a feline celebrity. He also became a professional "weather-cat." His predictions were printed regularly, and he did pretty well—about as accurate as human weather forecasters.

Why do cows have runny noses? It's the only part of their body that can sweat.

THE HEADLINE: *Vote for a Chimp, Not a Chump*
THE STAR: Tiao, a chimpanzee in Rio de Janeiro, Brazil
WHAT HAPPENED: Tiao was a main attraction at Rio's zoo, where he had a reputation for "losing his temper and throwing excrement at important people." In 1988 political activists formed the Brazilian Banana Party and ran Tiao for mayor as an anti-corruption candidate. He came in third, with more than 400,000 votes.
THE AFTERMATH: Tiao never ran for office again, but when he died in 1996, Rio's mayor declared a week-long mourning period and ordered all flags at the zoo be flown at half-mast. "It's a great loss," the mayor said. "He demonstrated the joyfulness of Rio."

THE HEADLINE: *Choking Kitten Calls 911, Saves Self*
THE STAR: Tipper, a cat in Tampa, Florida
WHAT HAPPENED: Tipper was home alone, chewing on his flea collar one afternoon in 1996, when he began choking on it. As he struggled to free it from his mouth, the cat somehow hit the phone's speed dial, which was programmed to dial the emergency number, 911. The dispatcher, hearing only meows, sent paramedics…who arrived minutes later. They found Tipper, removed the collar, and saved his life.
THE AFTERMATH: The story was featured on news programs all over the country. But three months later, Tipper disappeared from his owner's yard. When the owner called the county sheriff's office to report the missing cat, they told her, "Let's just hold tight and as soon as he gets to a phone, he'll call us."

ELEPHANT JOKES

We looked through our big gray trunk of jokes and found a whole bunch of elephants. Here they are.

Q: How do you get an elephant up an oak tree?
A: Plant an acorn under him and wait 50 years.

Q: How do you get an elephant down from an oak tree?
A: Tell her to sit on a leaf and wait until fall.

Q: What do you get when you cross an elephant and peanut butter?
A: Either peanut butter that never forgets or an elephant that sticks to the roof of your mouth.

How to sculpt an elephant: First, get a big block of marble, then chip away everything that doesn't look like an elephant.

Q: What did the grape say when the elephant sat on it?
A: Nothing, it just let out a little wine.

Q: How can you tell that an elephant has been in your fridge?
A: By the footprints in the butter.

An old man in France used to get up every morning and sprinkle white powder on the road. When asked what it was, he replied that it was special powder to keep the elephants away.

The person then remarked, "But there are no elephants in France!"

"See?" he said. "It works."

"Never eat more than you can lift." —*Miss Piggy*

COOL CARTOONS

More origins of your favorite animated shows.

ROCKET POWER

When Hungarian-born animator Gabor Csupo's kids were toddlers in 1989, he created a cartoon about them called *Rugrats*. Ten years later, Nickelodeon asked him for a new series. So he used his own children as an inspiration again and came up with stories about kids who are into extreme sports. The result: *Rocket Power*.

HEY ARNOLD!

• The football-headed Arnold was created by Seattle native Craig Bartlett. (He was originally a clay-mation character.)

• Nickelodeon was so impressed with Bartlett's work as a story editor on *Rugrats* that they decided to turn Arnold into an animated series in 1996.

• Bartlett learned a lot about cartooning from his brother-in-law, Matt Groening, creator of *The Simpsons*.

ED, EDD, N EDDY

Canadian cartoonist Danny Antonucci was handed the difficult task of coming up with a replacement for MTV's *Beavis and Butt-head*. So he created *The Grunts*. It flopped. Then he decided to try something completely different: a weird kids' show about weird kids. *Ed, Edd, N Eddy* premiered on the Cartoon Network in 1998.

Busy body: You make 200 billion new blood cells each day.

HOW TO READ
A DOLLAR BILL

*Looking for emergency bathroom reading the next time
you're without this book? Try a dollar bill. It's packed
with info, from the obvious to the symbolic.*

F IRST, THE BACK OF THE BILL...
• The pyramid stands for permanence and
strength. It's unfinished to represent the country's
future growth.

• The eye over the pyramid represents the overseeing
eye of God.

• The Latin phrase *Annuit Coeptis* above the pyramid
means "He Has Favored Our Undertakings."

• The Roman numeral MDCCLXXVI on the bottom
of the pyramid is the number 1776 (the year the U.S.
was founded).

One in five Americans cannot say which president is on the $1 bill without looking. Can you?

- *E Pluribus Unum* is a Latin phrase meaning "Out of Many, One" (50 states united into one nation).

- The eagle's head turns toward peace (symbolized by an olive branch); it turns away from war (represented by arrows). Check out how many olive leaves and arrows there are.

AND NOW, GEORGE'S SIDE OF THE BILL...

- First, a historical note: Ever wonder why George Washington's not smiling? Historians suspect it's because of his unattractive and ill-fitting false teeth.

- To the left of George is a letter in the center of a seal. That shows which Federal Reserve Bank issued the bill: Boston (A), New York (B), Philadelphia (C), Cleveland (D), Richmond (E), Atlanta (F), Chicago (G), St. Louis (H), Minneapolis (I), Kansas City (J), Dallas (K), or San Francisco (L).

- Below the seal is a series of numbers. This is the bill's serial number. Every bill has a different number.

- To the left of George is the signature of the Treasurer of the United States at the time the bill was printed.

One in 10 children sleepwalk.

THE SLAVE WHO SHIPPED HIMSELF TO FREEDOM

What's the cost of freedom? Here's the fascinating story of a man who risked his life to escape slavery.

IN HIS OWN WORDS

"I was born about forty-five miles from the city of Richmond [Virginia], in the year 1815. I entered the world a slave—in the midst of a country whose most honored writings declare that all men have a right to liberty."

Thus begins the extraordinary autobiography of a slave named Henry Brown, whose escape to freedom became famous in the years just before the Civil War.

ONE SLAVE AMONG MILLIONS

Brown's early life was no different from the lives of millions of other slaves in colonial America. His parents were slaves, so he was owned by whites from the moment of his birth.

Although Brown was treated better than most slaves, he was still not free. And how he saw his fellow slaves treated depressed him greatly. Brown wrote,

There are more creatures in your mouth than there are humans on Earth.

These Slaves were dressed in shirts made of coarse bagging such as coffee sacks are made from, and some kind of light substance for pantaloons [pants], and this was all their clothing! They had no shoes, hats, or coats.

Even more shameful was the constant physical and emotional torture that owners and overseers inflicted on their slaves. Brown wrote of one overseer:

> On one occasion I saw him take a slave, whose name was Pinkney, and make him take him off his shirt; he then gave him one hundred lashes on his bare back; and all this, because he lacked three pounds of his task, which was valued at six cents. I saw him do many other things which were equally cruel, but it would be [useless to list them—everyone] understands that slavery, even in its mildest forms, is a hard and cruel fate.

HAVING HIS OWN FAMILY

Eventually, Brown married a washerwoman slave named Nancy and they had several children. Nancy's owner promised that the family would never be separated. But he lied.

In 1848 the terrible day came when Henry learned that his wife and children were sold to a slave owner in another state. He wrote,

> No slave husband has any certainty whatever of being able to retain his wife a single hour; neither has any wife any more certainty of her husband: their fondest affection may be utterly disregarded, and their devoted attachment cruelly ignored at any moment a brutal slave-holder may think fit.

She with whom I had traveled the journey of life in chains, for the space of twelve years, and the dear little [children] God had given us I could see plainly were to be separated from me for ever, and I must continue, desolate and alone, to drag my chains through the world.

A BOLD PLAN

Desperate and disgusted, Brown came up with a plan.

One day, while I was at work, and my thoughts were eagerly feasting upon the idea of freedom, when the idea suddenly flashed across my mind of shutting myself up in a box, and getting myself conveyed as dry goods to a free state.

THIS SIDE UP, WITH CARE

It took the help of a sympathetic white shoemaker named Samuel Smith for Brown's plan to succeed. Smith built an innocent-looking shipping crate out of wood. It measured three feet long, two feet wide, and two and a half feet high—about half the size of an average car trunk. On March 23, 1849, Henry crammed his 200-pound body into it. Smith nailed the crate shut, leaving Henry in darkness…except for three small air holes. With only a sack of water and a few biscuits to keep him alive, Henry settled in for the long ride to freedom.

The journey was anything but easy. Even though the crate had been labeled "This Side Up, With Care," the box was tossed off wagons. More than once, Henry found himself upside down inside it.

More than 1,000 people belong to the Society of Jim Smiths. All of them are named Jim Smith.

REACHING FREEDOM

After a journey of 350 miles, which took 27 hours, the box arrived in Philadelphia, where waiting abolitionists (people determined to end slavery) collected it and took it to a safe place. Here is how Henry remembers what happened next:

A number of persons soon collected round the box after it was taken in to the house, but as I did not know what was going on I kept myself quiet. I heard a man say, "Let us rap upon the box and see if he is alive," and immediately a rap ensued and a voice said, tremblingly, "Is all right within?" to which I replied, "All right!"

The joy of the Friends [Quakers] was very great; when they heard that I was alive they soon managed to break open the box. I rose a freeman, but I was too weak, by reason of long confinement in that box, to be able to stand, so I immediately swooned away.

After my recovery, I had risen, as it were, from the dead. I felt much more than I could readily express; but as the kindness of Almighty God had been so conspicuously shown in my deliverance, I burst forth in [a song of] thanksgiving.

A BRIEF CELEBRITY

Embraced by the abolitionists, Henry toured the northern states of America, displaying the box and recounting his adventures to many people. People nicknamed him "Box" Brown—a name that would tag him for the rest of his life.

A LAST ESCAPE

But Brown's freedom was short-lived in the United States.

In 1850 Congress passed the Fugitive Slave Law, stating that any slave that ran away to freedom could be caught and returned to their master.

Refusing to return to slavery, "Box" Brown sailed to England. A year later, he published an autobiography, which sold many copies on both sides of the Atlantic and increased his fame. In England, he toured, speaking out against slavery.

In 1864, during the height of the American Civil War, he dropped from public sight. No one knows when or how he died. But it is safe to assume that Henry "Box" Brown died breathing the air of freedom.

It takes about 570 gallons of paint to paint the outside of the White House.

THE FIRST...

A few more fascinating firsts from our files.

T OOTHBRUSH
According to a 17th-century Chinese encyclopedia, the toothbrush was invented in China in 1498 and appears to have been of the same basic design as modern brushes. Toothbrush bristles were made from animal hair until 1938, when the first nylon-bristled brushes were introduced.

RADIO BROADCAST

The first radio broadcast was on Christmas Eve, 1906, in Brant Rock, Massachusetts. Professor Reginald Aubrey Fessenden played "O Holy Night" on the violin. The broadcast was heard as far away as the West Indies.

PARACHUTING

The first parachute jump from an aircraft was made by André-Jacques Garnerin on October 22, 1797. He jumped out of a balloon from a height of 2,230 feet and landed in a park in Paris. (The ride was so bumpy that he also became the first person to get airsick.)

FROZEN FOOD

The first individually packaged frozen food products were created by Clarence Birdseye. They first appeared at grocery stores in Springfield, Massachusetts, on March 6, 1930. Among the first products: frozen peas,

About 300 million people on Earth are left-handed. The rest (5.7 billion) are right-handed.

frozen spinach, frozen raspberries, and frozen fish.

ELEVATOR

The first passenger elevator was French, installed in King Louis XV's private rooms in the Palace of Versailles in 1743. The Flying Chair, as it was known, was actually on the outside of the building. And it had no motor—it went up and down with the assistance of a carefully balanced system of weights and pulleys.

COMICS

Before there were comic books, there were comic *strips*. The first was "The Yellow Kid," which appeared on Sundays in the *New York Journal* beginning on October 24, 1897. Daily comic strips started in 1904, and the first comic book was published in 1933 (it was a collection of comic strips).

RAINCOAT

The first raincoat was made by an engineer from French Guiana, François Fresnau. He discovered rubber trees there in 1747 and used their sap to waterproof an old overcoat by smearing it on.

HUMAN CANNONBALL

This feat was first performed at West's Amphitheatre in London, on April 2, 1877, by a performer named Zazel, billed as "A Beautiful Lady Fired from a Monstrous Cannon." The cannon was actually powered by springs, which gently "shot" her into a large safety net.

EVEN MORE GROSS STUFF

*More essential information about your body
and the gunk that comes out of it.*

*E*ARWAX
What's yellow and comes in little chunks like dried-up cheese or oozes out of your ear like Cheez Whiz? That's right: earwax. Besides keeping dirt, insects, and bacteria from creeping down your ear canal and damaging your eardrum, earwax also keeps cold air from blasting into your head. Ever see a picture of the inside of an ear? It looks like a long tunnel with an eardrum at the end. Tiny little hairs line the entrance to the auditory canal (the tunnel) and are the first line of defense, keeping dirt and other bad stuff out of your ear.

In addition to the hairs, your auditory canal has more than 4,000 wax-producing glands. The wax helps trap bacteria and dirt. Of course your ear, like every other part of your body, also sheds dead skin. So mix the dead skin with fresh wax, add some sweat and a little oil from your glands, and you've got a nice glop of yellow earwax. This wax flows like lava out to the opening of the ear, where it dries up, flakes, and falls onto your collar. Eww!

What makes the horseshoe crab unique? It's the only animal that chews food with its legs.

BELLY BUTTON LINT

There you are in your cute little bathing suit, draped across a big towel on a beautiful beach. You look down and—*embarrassment!*—your belly button is filled with some kind of grayish-greenish stuff. What IS that? Well, that stuff is dead skin cells—the main ingredient for toe jam, too (see page 119).

The difference here is in the navel itself. You see, a belly button looks like the knotted part of a balloon, with lots of tiny folds and tucks. When your skin sloughs off dead cells, which it does all the time, those cells usually float off into the air. But in your belly button, they get trapped inside all the little folds of skin. Add a little body sweat, and those folds get moist and warm. Next thing you know, those dead cells are gooey and starting to rot. That's what makes belly button lint so smelly! Add some stray fibers from your underwear or shirt, and you've got a fuzzy navel.

*   *   *

THE BRAIN FAMILY QUIZ

Marie Brain's father has five daughters:

1. Chacha, 2. Cheche, 3. Chichi, 4. Chocho, 5. ????

What is the fifth daughter's name?

Answer:

Marie

What did American kids eat for breakfast in 1776? Popcorn served with sugar and cream.

SOMETHING ABOUT "MARY"

Here are details about the battle between two New England towns that each claim to be the birthplace of the legendary poem "Mary Had a Little Lamb."

WHO WROTE THE POEM?

Theory #1: A schoolboy named John Roulstone in Sterling, Massachusetts. He was visiting a classroom in Sterling one day in 1815, when a pet lamb followed its owner—a girl named Mary Sawyer—to school. When the teacher called Mary to the front of the class, the lamb followed her up the aisle. Roulstone was so amused that he jotted down the first three stanzas of "Mary Had a Little Lamb."

Evidence: In an 1879 letter, Mary Sawyer described the schoolroom incident and credited Roulstone with writing the poem. This version of the story has been widely accepted for more than a century.

Theory #2: A nationally known writer and editor named Sarah Josepha Hale wrote the poem in Newport, New Hampshire (70 miles north of Sterling) in 1830. Hale, editor of *Godey's Lady's Book* (a women's magazine), was the author of over 20 books and hundreds of poems.

Evidence: Hale, who also helped make Thanksgiving a

national holiday, published "Mary Had a Little Lamb" under her own name in 1830 in a publication called *Poems for Our Children*. Then in 1889, shortly before she died, she signed a statement claiming authorship.

Supporters say that she was simply too distinguished to falsely claim ownership of a poem she had not written. "Why would she stoop to plagiarize a children's poem?" says Hale enthusiast Andrea Thorpe.

BUT REALLY, WHY DOES IT MATTER?

Why make a big deal out of who wrote the poem? Apparently, it's the primary claim to fame of both Newport *and* Sterling, so residents of those towns have a lot at stake. According to a 1998 article in the *Boston Globe*, they're trying to preserve three things:

1. Tourist Dollars

Sterling: The town "promotes itself as the home of Mary and her lamb. A small bronze lamb statue stands in tribute on the town square. The Sterling Historical Society sells Mary's lamb T-shirts and note cards and fuzzy lamb statuettes."

• In 1999 Sterling formed the Mary's Little Lamb Association, hoping to raise $250,000 in donations—enough to restore Mary Sawyer's original farmhouse and turn it into a historical monument.

Newport: "Like Sterling, Newport proudly displays its link to the lamb. A memorial plaque to Hale states that 'she composed the poem now called "Mary Had a Little Lamb."' Tour guides talk about it, and it's a subject of the Newport information guide produced by the Chamber of Commerce."

2. A Native Daughter's Reputation

Sterling: If Hale really did write the poem, then Mary Sawyer—Sterling's pride and joy—was a liar. Mary's sixth-generation relative (and Sterling resident) Diane Melone won't have any of that. But she is willing to agree that Hale may have written the last three verses.

Newport: However, that would mean Hale didn't write the whole thing…so *she*'d be a liar. That's completely unacceptable to Hale-ites in Newport. "Like she needs to be given the last three verses," says Andrea Thorpe. "We have no doubt that Sarah wrote it.…Everyone except Sterling agrees with me."

3. Local Pride

Sterling: "Everybody knew [the poem is part of Sterling

There are 140 towns and cities in the U.S. that have the word "Christmas" in their names.

history]," says Melone. Denying it is "like living in Gettysburg and saying the Battle of Gettysburg didn't happen there."

Newport: From her office in New Hampshire, Thorpe monitors the national scene. Whenever she discovers that someone has taken Sterling's side, she sends "a standard indignant letter": "Your article about the authorship of the poem 'Mary's Lamb' shows a complete disregard for literary history…and an ignorance of the contributions made by one of the most famous people to come from Newport."

UPDATE

Meanwhile, two scholars—Lee Swanson and B. G. Thurston—are involved in a research project that could undermine *both* claims.

They've traced the history of "Mary Had a Little Lamb" to back before Roulstone or Hale. Linda Matchan of the *Boston Globe* reports that "their research has led them to a nearly identical British version of the poem, published earlier than Hale's, about a 'Lucy' and her little lamb." They are in the process of verifying the information.

"Where would this leave Sterling and Newport?" Matchan asks. "A little sheepish perhaps?"

"I don't know," says Thurston. "I truly believe neither side is correct, though I don't have the full research to support it. It might be one of those mysteries that will never be solved."

Sheep snore.

A HISTORY OF THE YO-YO, PART II

Here's the rest of our brief history of one of the world's oldest and most popular toys. (The first part is on page 83.)

SALES HYPE

Donald Duncan took the yo-yo, an ancient toy, and turned it into a modern marvel. He started manufacturing an improved version of the yo-yo in 1929 with a "sleeper string" which made it possible to do yo-yo tricks.

But it took more than a technical innovation to make the yo-yo a national fad. It took promotion—and Duncan was an advertising genius. Here are some of the stunts he created:

• **Yo-yo Champions.** Many Filipinos living in the United States had played with yo-yos since they were kids. Duncan hired 42 of them, gave them each the title "Champion," and sent them on a national tour to demonstrate—and sell—yo-yos.

• **Yo-yo contests.** Duncan sponsored neighborhood yo-yo contests all over the country, awarding new yo-yos, "All-American Yo-Yo Sweaters," baseballs, gloves, bicycles, and other prizes to winners. He even got newspaper owner William Randolph Hearst to publicize the contests (in exchange, Duncan required all

---

"Knock knock." "Who's there?" "Ya." "Ya who?" "I didn't know you were a cowboy!"

contestants to sell three newspaper subscriptions each).

• **Celebrity yo-yo endorsements.** Duncan photographed actors, athletes, and other celebrities playing with yo-yos. Two of the first who agreed to the photos were Hollywood's biggest stars—Douglas Fairbanks and Mary Pickford (today's equivalent: Tom Cruise and Julia Roberts).

The promotions paid off. By the early 1930s, annual sales had shot from thousands of yo-yos to millions.

WHOSE NAME IS IT, ANYWAY?

But the biggest yo-yo craze in history took place in the 1960s. In 1962 alone, according to news reports, 45 million were sold—despite the fact that there were only 40 million kids in the country. This should have been the Duncan Yo-Yo Company's finest hour—but it was their undoing. Why? One reason was that they lost their "yo-yo" trademark.

There was so much money to be made that other companies wanted to use the name, too, so they challenged the trademark in court. They pointed to a billboard near the Duncan factory: "Welcome to the Yo-Yo Capital of the World." Well, if there was a yo-yo capital, that must mean yo-yos were made elsewhere, too. In 1962 a federal court ruled that the trademark was invalid—the word *yo-yo* was the name of the toy itself.

This, combined with increasing costs and competition from Frisbees, skateboards, and other toys, sent the company into a tailspin. In 1965 the Duncan Company, which was responsible for making the yo-yo an international craze, filed for bankruptcy. But who knows? Maybe, just like a yo-yo, the fad will "come come" back again.

YO-YO FACTS

• Donald Duncan applied his promotional genius to other products: he also invented the Eskimo Pie, originated the Good Humor ice cream truck, and was the first person to successfully market the parking meter.

• In the early 1900s, Hubert Meyer of Toledo, Ohio, patented an *edible* yo-yo.

• In 1984 astronaut David Griggs brought a yo-yo on board the Space Shuttle as part of NASA's "Toys in Space" experiments. His finding: yo-yos don't "sleep" in space—they just reach the end of their string and bounce right back up.

• The world's record for yo-yoing was set by John Winslow of Gloucester, Virginia. He started on November 23, 1977 and didn't stop for five days— 120 hours.

• The world's largest yo-yo, Big-Yo, is 50" tall and $31\frac{1}{2}$" wide, and weighs 256 pounds. The string is $\frac{3}{4}$" braided Dacron rope. In 1980 the *You Asked for It* TV show launched it off Pier 39 in San Francisco. But the string accidentally got wet before the launch, so Big-Yo kept spinning in a "sleeper" position until its axle overheated and the string burned through. The huge yo-yo plunged 30 feet into San Francisco Bay, and scuba divers had to keep it from drifting away until it could be retrieved and towed to shore.

MR. MOONLIGHT

What is a moon? It's a natural satellite which orbits a planet.
Here are some facts about our big night-light in the sky.

• It takes 29 days, 12 hours, 44 minutes, and 3 seconds for the moon to go through all of its phases (from one full moon to the next). This is close to the length of a month—which is why the word *month* comes from *moon.*

• The light that seems to come from the moon is really sunlight reflected off the moon's surface. It takes 1.25 seconds for the light to travel to Earth.

• The moon is 2,160 miles in diameter—about a quarter of Earth's diameter.

• Since the moon spins once on its axis every 27⅓ days—the same amount of time it takes to go around Earth once—we only see one side of it.

• The temperature range on the moon is –383°F to 231°F.

• More than 843 pounds of moon samples have been brought back to Earth.

• There is no sound on the moon. Nor is there weather, wind, clouds, or colors at sunrise and sunset.

• If you weigh 120 pounds on Earth, you would weigh 20 pounds on the moon—one-sixth of your Earth weight.

• Earth's gravity keeps the moon in its orbit, but the moon pulls back, too. The result: ocean tides. But it's not just the oceans that are affected: land masses get "bloated" when the moon is directly overhead.

Your blood is 83% water, your brain is 74% water, and your bones are 22% water.

AMAZING KIDS

This courageous kid defied danger to set a world record.

THE TEEN WHO REACHED THE TOP
At 29,035 feet, Mt. Everest in Nepal is the tallest spot on the planet. No one was able to climb it until 1953, when Edmund Hillary and Tenzing Norgay became the first. Since then, it has become the ultimate mountain climb. Now more than 1,400 people have made it to the top, including a 15-year-old eighth-grader from Nepal named Temba Tsheri.

It took Temba two tries. On his first attempt, in 2000, he was forced to turn back only 160 feet from the summit. You see, Temba made the mistake of opening his gloves to tie his shoes. That sounds reasonable, but he left his gloves off for 45 minutes...and it cost him. By the time he got off the mountain, five of his fingers turned black from frostbite and had to be amputated.

IF AT FIRST YOU DON'T SUCCEED...

But that didn't stop him; the following year, he and his team tried again...and made it. On May 23, 2001, Temba became the youngest person ever to climb Mt. Everest.

But should kids be allowed to risk their lives this way? The government of Nepal doesn't think so. In 2002, they passed a law banning anyone under age 16 from climbing the mountain, which means Temba's record will probably last forever.

Animal fact: The food a sloth eats today won't be fully digested until two weeks from now.

BATHROOM LORE

*More history of the room you
might be sitting in right now.*

A FEW AMERICAN FIRSTS
• First toilet in the White House: Installed for John Quincy Adams in 1825 leading to a new slang term for toilet—a *quincy*.

• First city with modern waterworks: Philadelphia, 1820.

• First city with a modern sewage system: Boston, 1823.

THE FIRST TOILET PAPER

• In ancient times, there was no toilet paper. Well-to-do Romans used sponges or wool, with rosewater. Everyone else used whatever was at hand, including sticks, stones, leaves, and dry bones.

• Toilet paper was introduced in America in 1857, as a package of loose sheets. But it was too much like the paper Americans already used for the purpose at that time—the Sears catalog. It flopped.

• In 1879 an Englishman named Walter Alcock created the first perforated rolls of toilet paper. A year later, Philadelphia's Scott brothers introduced Waldorf Tissue, which was discreetly sold in unlabeled brown wrappers... so that buyers wouldn't be embarrassed asking for it.

The wingspan of a 747 (213 feet) is longer than the Wright brothers first flight (120 feet).

THE SWORD OF DAMOCLES

Here's one of Uncle John's favorite ancient Greek myths.

There was once a rich and powerful Greek king named Dionysius. A clever, ruthless man, Dionysius had fought his way to the throne and he'd made many powerful and bitter enemies. Yet there were some who envied Dionysius and wished they were in his place.

Among the king's courtiers was a man named Damocles. Damocles was constantly praising Dionysius and saying, "Oh great king, you are magnificent. The gods smile upon you. Everything you wish for is yours. How happy and content you must be!"

One day, as Damocles was speaking in his usual flattering way, Dionysius said, "What are you saying Damocles? Would you like to be king in my place?"

Damocles didn't want the king to think he was plotting to seize the throne, so he quickly replied, "Oh no, great king. I was only thinking how wonderful it would be to enjoy your riches for even one day."

"So shall it be," said King Dionysius. "For one day, you shall enjoy the power and luxury of a king. And you will know exactly what it feels like to be in my place."

The next day Damocles was led into the king's bedroom. There, the king's servants dressed Damocles in royal robes, led him to the king's throne, and told him that he could do whatever he wished.

Suddenly, Damocles gasped with horror. Just above his head was an enormous sword hanging by a slender thread! If the thread broke, the sword would instantly fall and kill him. Pointing to the sword in terror, he whispered, "That sword! Why is that sword hanging above me?"

"I promised you," answered Dionysius, "that you

would know exactly how it feels to live like a king, and now you know! Did you expect that you would enjoy all of the king's riches and pay no price? Don't you know that I always live with a sword hanging over my head? I must be on my guard every moment lest I be slain."

Then Damocles answered, "Oh king, take back your wealth and your power! I would not have it for another moment. I would rather be a poor peasant living in a mountain hut than live in fear and trembling all the days of my life!"

Never again did Damocles envy the king.

FAMOUS FOR BEING NAKED

We know—this sounds a little weird, butt…er…we mean but…it's just another way to look at history.

L ADY GODIVA, wife of Earl Leofric, lord of Coventry, England, in the 1100s

Famous for: Riding horseback through Coventry, covered only by her long blonde hair.

The Bare Facts: Lady Godiva was upset by the heavy taxes her husband had imposed on poor people in his domain. When she asked him to give the folks a break, he laughingly replied that he'd cut the taxes if she would ride through the town naked. To his shock, she agreed. But she requested that townspeople stay indoors and not peek while she rode through the streets. Legend has it that they all complied except for one young man named Tom, who secretly watched through a shutter…which gave us the term "peeping Tom."

ARCHIMEDES (287–212 B.C.), one of the most brilliant thinkers of the Ancient World

Famous for: Running naked through the streets of ancient Syracuse, screaming "Eureka!"

The Bare Facts: King Hieron II of Syracuse, Sicily, was suspicious that his new crown wasn't solid gold. Had

When dogs and humans sleep together, they dream at the same times during the night.

the goldsmith secretly mixed in some silver? He asked Archimedes to find out.

Archimedes studied the crown. He weighed it; then he weighed a piece of pure gold identical to the piece the goldsmith had been given. Sure enough, they weighed the same. Archimedes still wasn't sure, and he thought about it for days.

Then one evening, as Archimedes lowered himself into his bathtub, water overflowed onto the floor and he suddenly knew the answer. He jumped out of the tub, and forgetting that he was naked, he ran down the street to the palace shouting, "Eureka!" ("I have found it!")

Archimedes later explained his discovery to the king: "When an object is placed in water," he said, "it displaces an amount of water equal to its own volume."

To demonstrate, he put the crown in a bowl of water and measured the overflow. Then he put a lump of gold that weighed the same as the crown into the bowl. When the water was measured, the King saw that the gold had spilled less than the crown. It was proof that the goldsmith really had tried to cheat the king. The secret: Silver is lighter than gold, so to make up the correct weight, extra silver was needed. That meant the volume of the crown was slightly more than the gold, so the crown spilled more water.

Archimedes became famous for his discovery. We can only guess what happened to the goldsmith.

RED BUTTONS, a popular red-headed actor of the 1940s and 1950s

Q: Why does honey give you energy quickly?   A: It's already been digested once—by the bees.

Famous for: Being the first person ever to appear naked on TV.

The Bare Facts: In the early 1950s, Buttons appeared on the *Milton Berle Show*, which was broadcast live (in those days there was no videotape, so all shows were broadcast live).

They were doing a skit, which featured Berle as a doctor and Buttons as a shy patient who wouldn't disrobe for his exam. Buttons wore a special "breakaway" suit—the coat, shirt, and pants were sewn together so they'd all come off when Berle yanked on the shirt collar. As he explained in *The Hollywood Walk of Shame*:

> When my character refused to get undressed, Milton was supposed to grab my shirtfront and rip the entire thing off—and I'd be left standing there in old-fashioned, knee-to-neck one-piece underwear. That was the laugh.
>
> Well, Milton accidentally grabbed me *under* the collar. And when he yanked at my breakaway suit, everything came off—including my underwear! We were on live television and there I stood—nude in front of a studio audience and all the people watching at home. When I realized what had happened, I got behind Milton, who was as shocked as I was, but had the presence of mind to announce the next act and have the curtain closed.

Buttons added: "I turned as red as my hair."

* * *

Random Fact: The Nintendo Company is more than a century old. Its first product was playing cards.

Ha Ha! Q: Why was the broom late for school? A: It over swept.

AESOP'S FABLES

Aesop's fables have been told and retold for thousands of years. Here are a few we thought you'd like.

THE FOX & THE GRAPES

A fox was walking along the road when he spied some delicious-looking grapes growing

on a high trellis. "My, they look good!" he said. He jumped up, but couldn't reach them. He tried again and again, but to no avail. Finally he looked angrily at the grapes and said, "Hmmm, who wants the old grapes? They're probably sour anyway."

Moral: *It's easy to despise what you can't have.*

THE SICK LION

A lion, unable from old age and infirmities to provide himself with food by force, resolved to do so by trickery. He returned to his den and, lying down there, pretended to be sick, taking care that his sickness should be publicly known. The beasts expressed their sorrow, and came one by one to

---

An elephant's brain weighs about four times as much as a human's brain.

his den, where the lion devoured them.

After many of the beasts had thus disappeared, a fox, presenting himself to the lion, stood on the outside of the cave, at a respectful distance, and asked him how he was. "I am very middling," replied the lion, "but why are you standing out there? Please come in and talk with me." "No, thank you," said the fox. "I notice that there are many footprints entering your cave, but I see no trace of any returning."

Moral: *The wise person learns from the misfortunes of others.*

THE FOOLISH TRAVELERS

A man and his son were walking along the road to market with their donkey. As they walked, they met a couple. "Did you ever see anything so silly?" the man said to his wife. "Two men walking when they have a donkey with them. What's a donkey for, after all, if not to carry a man?"

Hearing this, the man put his son on the back of the donkey and they went on their way. Soon they met two countrymen. "Did you ever see such a terrible thing?" one cried. "The strong young man rides while his poor father must walk." So the boy dismounted and the father got on instead.

They hadn't gone very much farther when they met two women. "Look at that heartless father!" exclaimed one of them, "His poor little son must walk while he rides." At that, the man said to his son, "Come up here with me. We'll both ride."

They both rode for a while until they reached a group of men. "Aren't you ashamed," they called out. "Overloading a poor little donkey like that." So the man and his son both climbed off the donkey.

They thought and thought. They couldn't walk along with the donkey, or ride it one at a time, or ride it both together. Then they had an idea. They got a tree and cut it into a long pole. Then they tied the donkey's feet to it, raised the pole to their shoulders, and went on their way, carrying the donkey.

As they crossed a bridge, the donkey—who didn't like being tied up—kicked one of his feet loose, causing the father and son to stumble. The donkey fell into the water. And because its feet were tied...it drowned.

Moral: *If you try to please everyone, you'll end up pleasing no one.*

THE THIRSTY PIGEON

A pigeon, overcome by thirst, saw a glass of water painted on a sign. Not realizing it was only a picture, she quickly flew toward it and crashed into the sign. Her wings broken, she fell to the ground...and was captured by an onlooker.

Moral: *Don't let enthusiasm cloud your judgment.*

THE DONKEY & THE FOX

A donkey put on a lion's skin and roamed around the forest amusing himself by scaring all the foolish animals he met. Finally, he met a fox and tried to scare him, too—but as soon as the fox heard the donkey's voice, he said, "Well, I might have been frightened...if I hadn't heard your bray."

Moral: *Clothes may disguise a fool, but his words give him away.*

---

20 million bats live in Texas's Bracken Cave. They eat 100 tons of insects every night.

UNCLE JOHN'S GENIUS QUIZ

Ready for a challenge? Have fun with these puzzles.

1. It's A-maze-ing. Using a pencil, can you trace a continuous path along all five squares without stopping, without going over the same segment twice, and without crossing a line you've already laid down?

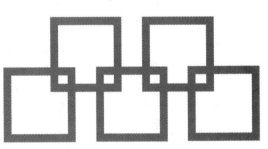

2. Row! Row! Row! Can you move just one coin to make two rows of five coins each?

Answers on page 283.

British anatomist Richard Owen invented the word *dinosaur* in 1841.

ZAPPED!

*Some of the scariest and most mysterious natural
phenomena are the crack of thunder and the
flash of lightning. But what are they?*

LIKE A BOLT OUT OF THE BLUE

Every second of the day, about 100 bolts of lightning strike someplace on Earth. That adds up to almost 8 million strikes a day. And each bolt has an electrical charge of 100 million to one billion volts. That's enough electricity to light up a small town for an entire year!

The Vikings believed lightning struck every time the thunder god Thor threw his hammer. But what *really* happens?

First, tiny drops of water or ice start rubbing together inside giant storm clouds, kind of like Boy Scouts rubbing two sticks together to start a fire. This rubbing action knocks electrons off the water molecules, which gives the cloud an electrical charge. When the electrical charge gets big enough, giant sparks (lightning) burst out of the clouds. That burst of energy heats the air so quickly that it causes the air to actually explode, creating a big boom (thunder).

STRIKING OUT

Lightning can leap from one cloud to another, or from a cloud to the ground and then back again. It travels so

---

Most armadillos have four babies at a time. They're always identical quadruplets.

fast that many sparks appear to be a single flash. Lightning and thunder occur at the same time, but because light travels faster than sound, they seem like separate events (you always see the lightning before you hear the thunder). You can never have thunder without lightning, and, despite what people say, lightning *can* strike the same place twice. The Empire State Building has been struck as many as 12 times in one 20-minute storm. It gets about 500 strikes a year.

BE CAREFUL!

Worried about being zapped by a lightning bolt? You should be—lightning is responsible for more than a hundred deaths a year in the U.S. and Canada alone. Here are a few tips for avoiding a confrontation with lightning:

• First, watch out in Florida, Texas, and North Carolina. Those states have the greatest number of deaths by lightning. Especially avoid them in June—the worst month for lightning.

• And as long as you're avoiding places…if a thunderstorm starts, stay away from open spaces like fields and golf courses. Lightning tends to strike the highest point it can find, and in an open field, the highest point might be you.

• Being in or around swimming pools, lakes, or other bodies of water during a storm is a bad idea, too.

• If you're caught in a thunderstorm, run for cover… but not under a tree. The safest place to be is inside a

---

233 dalmatians were used in the filming of the movie *101 Dalmatians*.

building—especially a building with a lightning rod. Lightning strikes the rod and follows it straight down to the ground, instead of going into the building and zapping you. Who figured that out? Benjamin Franklin. And yup, he did it with a kite and a key.

• Another safe place to hide is in a car (no convertibles, please!). Roll up the windows and be sure not to touch the metal parts.

• And remember—lightning can strike as far as 20 miles away from a storm. So if there is blue sky above you but a storm in the distance, head indoors.

• Sometimes people can tell when lightning is about to strike—the hair on their arms or head stands up. Seriously. Put your arm next to a TV screen and you may get a buzzy electrical feeling. That's what people describe feeling just before a lightning strike. So if you get that feeling in a storm, find a hiding place.

• If there's no place to hide, quickly take the lightning safety position.

LIGHTNING SAFETY POSITION

Some people might tell you to lie flat on the ground in a lightning storm, but they're wrong. Lightning can travel along the ground and you *don't* want to be in its path!

The best thing to do is squat with your heels together and your hands over your ears. This makes you look a little like the "hear no evil" monkey, but it also makes you safer.

When you're squatting, you are a smaller target. And

American tables are set with salt and pepper; in Hungary, it's salt and paprika.

with your heels together, the lightning will go up one leg, down the other leg, and back into the ground—not into your body and through your heart. You cover your ears to protect them from the deafening explosion.

THUNDER AND LIGHTNING FACTS

• The air near a lightning strike is greater than 50,000°F—hotter than the surface of the sun.

• A thunderstorm has more explosive power than an atomic bomb.

• Inside information: On rare occasions, lightning has been known to enter houses through phone lines and water pipes.

• In 1998 lightning in the Congo killed an entire soccer team of 11 players. In 1999 lightning injured a whole football team in Colorado.

• Bogor, Java, is the record holder for the place with the most lightning. It has lightning 322 days out of the year.

• Your chance of being struck by lightning is 1 in 600,000.

England is only two-thirds the size of New England.

EVEN STEVEN

Who is Uncle John's favorite comedian? Steven Wright.

"Right now, I'm having amnesia and déjà vu at the same time. I think I've forgotten this before."

"I put tape on the mirrors in my house so I don't accidentally walk through into another dimension."

"I spilled spot remover on my dog and now he's gone."

"I bought some batteries, but they weren't included...so I had to buy them again."

"I installed a skylight in my apartment. The people who live above me are furious."

"If you were going to shoot a mime, would you use a silencer?"

"I have the world's largest collection of seashells. I keep it on the beaches of the world. Perhaps you've seen it."

"I locked my keys in the car the other day. But it was all right. I was still inside."

"I had amnesia once... or twice."

"I'm writing a book. I've got the page numbers done, so now I just have to fill up the rest."

"I walked into a restaurant. The sign said 'Breakfast Served— Any Time.' I ordered French toast...during the Renaissance."

"I used to work in a fire hydrant factory. You couldn't park anywhere near the place."

In their first year of life, puppies grow 10 times faster than human infants do.

IT'S A WEIRD, WEIRD WORLD

Proof that truth really is stranger than fiction.

MIDNIGHT SWIM
"Freddie Padgett was so terrified of water that he wore a life jacket to bed on stormy nights. Friends made fun of him…until a twister sucked him out of his RV while he was sleeping and dropped him into a lake over a mile away. He suffered broken ribs, but authorities say the life jacket actually saved his life."

—*The Skeptic*

NOSING AROUND

"Ruth Clarke of London underwent surgery to correct a lifelong breathing problem in 1981. She was presented with a tiddlywink, which doctors removed from her nose. Clarke vaguely recalled losing the disk as a tot, but never dreamed it was right under her nose the whole time."

—*Encyclopedia Brown's Book of Strange Facts*

THE POSTMAN RINGS MORE THAN TWICE

"From 1974 to 1976, a young man in Taiwan wrote 700 love letters to his girlfriend, trying to talk her into marriage. He succeeded—she married the mailman who delivered the letters to her."

—*Weird News and Strange Stories*

Mark Twain coined the term "gossip column" in 1893.

RABBIT BRINGS FIRE TO THE PEOPLE

This Native American folklore from the Creek tribe explains how they acquired fire.

In the beginning, there was no fire and Earth was cold. Then the Thunderbirds sent their lightning to a sycamore tree on an island where the Weasels lived. The Weasels were the only ones who had fire and they would not give any of it away.

The people knew that there was fire on the island because they could see smoke coming from the sycamore, but the water was too deep for anyone to cross. When winter came, the people suffered so much from the cold that they called a council to find some way of obtaining fire from the Weasels. They invited all the animals who could swim.

"How shall we obtain fire?" the people asked.

Most of the animals were afraid of the Weasels

because they were blood-thirsty and ate mice and moles and fish and birds. Rabbit was the only one who was brave enough to try to steal fire from them. "I can run and swim faster than the Weasels," he said. "I am also a good dancer."

"Every night the Weasels build a big fire and dance around it. Tonight I will swim across and join in the dancing. I will run away with some fire."

He considered the matter for a while and then decided how he would do it. Before the sun set he rubbed his head with pine tar to make his hair stand up. Then, as darkness was falling, he swam across to the island.

The Weasels received Rabbit gladly because they had heard of his fame as a dancer. Soon they had a big fire blazing and all began dancing around it. As the Weasels danced, they approached nearer and nearer the fire in the center of the circle. They would bow to the fire and then dance backward away from it.

When Rabbit entered the dancing circle, the Weasels shouted to him: "Lead us, Rabbit!" He danced ahead of them, coming closer and closer to the fire. He bowed to the fire, bringing his head lower and lower as if he were going to take hold of it. While the Weasels were dancing faster and faster, trying to keep up with him, Rabbit suddenly bowed very low so that the pine tar in his hair caught fire in a flash of flame.

There's only one kind of wild rabbit in the U.S.: the cottontail. All the rest are hares.

He ran off with his head ablaze, and the angry Weasels pursued him, crying, "Catch him! Catch him! He has stolen our sacred fire! Catch him, and throw him down!"

But Rabbit outran them and plunged into the water, leaving the Weasels on the shore. He swam across the water with the flames still blazing from his hair.

The Weasels now called on the Thunderbirds to make it rain so as to extinguish the fire stolen by Rabbit. For three days rain poured down upon the Earth, and the Weasels were sure that no fire was left burning except in their sycamore tree.

Rabbit, however, had built a fire in a hollow log, and when the rain stopped and the sun shone, he came out and gave fire to all the people. After that, whenever it rained, they kept fires in their shelters, and that is how Rabbit brought fire to the people.

Poll result: 58% of schoolkids say pizza is their favorite cafeteria food.

WHAT'S IN A NAME?

*You already know these names. After reading
this, you'll know where they came from.*

SONY. In 1958 company founder Akio Morita
wanted a name he could market internationally.
He looked through a Latin dictionary, picked out
the word *sonus* ("sound"), and combined it with
"sonny" (as in sonny-boy).

CHEERIOS. Originally called CherriOats. In 1946
Quaker Oats threatened to sue, claiming it had exclusive rights to the name "Oats." Rather than fight, General Mills switched to Cheerios.

CONVERSE ALL-STARS. Named for Marquis M.
Converse, who founded the Converse Rubber Company
in 1908. He introduced the canvas-topped All-Star—
one of the world's first basketball shoes—in 1917.

GREY POUPON DIJON MUSTARD. Named for the
Englishman who invented it—Maurice Grey—and his
French business partner—Auguste Poupon—who put up
money to open a mustard factory in...Dijon, France.

CARNATION. In 1901, while walking down a street
in Seattle, the head of the Pacific Coast Condensed
Milk Company noticed a box of Carnation Brand cigars
in a store window. He decided it would make a good
name for his milk, too. He put a picture of a flower on
the label so it would be recognizable even to children.

THE REMOTE CONTROL

*More than 400 million TV remote controls
are currently in use in the United States.
Here's the story of their creation.*

T HE FIRST TV REMOTES
• Commander Eugene MacDonald, Jr., president of the Zenith Radio Co., hated TV commercials. He figured other Americans did, too, so he told his researchers to create a system that would mute all ads by remote control.

• Zenith wasn't the only one working on this idea. Another company introduced a TV remote control that operated with radio waves. Unfortunately, the waves traveled through walls and down the street, so they tended to operate *neighbors'* TV sets as well.

TRY, TRY AGAIN

• In the early 1950s, Zenith developed two remote-control systems, both of which flopped:

1. The Lazy Bones connected to the TV with a long cable. It worked, but among other problems, it kept tripping people.

2. The more advanced Flash-Matic used four photocells, one in each corner of a TV cabinet. Each cell

---

Finger used most for nose picking: index finger (65.1%). Least: thumb (16.4%).

controlled one function—volume, channels, and so on. All a viewer had to do was aim a flashlight at the right cell. Unfortunately, first-generation couch potatoes couldn't remember which cell did what…and direct sunlight operated all of them at once!

• In 1955 Robert Adler, a Zenith acoustics expert, developed a remote system using high-frequency sound. The device contained a miniature aluminum rod that rang when hit by a hammer. Called the Space Commander 200, it debuted in 1956. Retail price: $399.95. Unfortunately, any noises produced by small pieces of metal, such as jingling keys or dog chains, were similar to the remote's, so channels changed and sets turned on and off unpredictably.

AT LAST!

• By 1962 the kinks in the Space Commander were worked out. Bulky vacuum tubes were replaced with transistors, making the remote smaller and cheaper. Adler's development of ultrasound remained the technique for all remote controls until the early 1980s, when new semiconductors (silicon chips) made infrared remote controls capable of transmitting digital codes. And that's still how remotes work today.

Some beaver dams are more than 1,000 years old.

A BRIEF HISTORY OF BUGS BUNNY

Who's your favorite cartoon character? Ear's ours.

BACKGROUND
It took Warner Bros. many years to develop Bugs.
• In 1937 animation director Tex Avery made "Porky's Duck Hunt," in which Porky Pig hunted a screwball duck named Daffy.

• A year later, Warner Bros. director Ben "Bugs" Hardaway remade the cartoon with a rabbit instead of a duck, as "Porky's Hare Hunt." Says one of Bugs's creators: "That rabbit was just Daffy Duck in a rabbit suit."

• In 1939 Hardaway made a new version as "Hare-um Scare-um"…with a new rabbit. Cartoonist Charlie Thorson came up with a gray-and-white buck-toothed rabbit. He labeled his sketches "Bugs' Bunny."

• In 1940 Tex Avery made "A Wild Hare," the cartoon that made Bugs what he is today: a smart-aleck rabbit, always in command in the face of danger. And it was Avery who gave him the line "What's up, Doc?"

INSPIRATIONS
But is that Bugs' true origin? Cartoon historians say his ancestry goes further back. A few direct ancestors:

• **Zomo.** You may not have heard of this African folk

---

rabbit, but he was world-famous. Joe Adamson writes in *Bugs Bunny: Fifty Years and Only One Grey Hare*:

> Like jazz and rock 'n' roll, Bugs has at least some of his roots in black culture. Zomo is the trickster rabbit from Central and Eastern Africa who gained audience sympathy by being smaller than his oppressors and turning the tables on them through cleverness. He was a con artist, a masquerader, ruthless and suave, always in control of the situation.

• **B'rer Rabbit.** Slaves brought Zomo to the New World where he became known as Br'er Rabbit, whose stories were retold by Joel Chandler Harris in Uncle Remus books (1880–1906). Typical plot: Br'er Fox catches Br'er Rabbit, who begs not to be thrown in the briar patch (which is exactly where he wants to go because then he can escape). Br'er Fox falls for it, tosses him in, and the rabbit laughs all the way home. Occasionally, Bugs pulls the same trick.

A couple of comedic geniuses also influenced Bugs:

• **Charlie Chaplin.** Looney Tunes directors, all fans of Chaplin, stole a lot of his gags. For example, Adamson writes, "the abrupt and shocking kiss Charlie plants on someone who's getting too close for comfort in *The Floorwalker* went on to become one of Bugs's favorite ways to upset his adversaries."

• **Groucho Marx.** "Bugs uses his carrot as a prop, as Groucho used his cigar," writes Stefan Kanfer in *Serious Business*. "Eventually Bugs even stole Marx's response to an insult: 'Of course you know, this means war!' "

Do you dream in color? According to one source, only 5% of Americans do.

TRADEMARKS

Why Carrot-Crunching? No one's sure where it came from, but some people think it might have been taken from Frank Capra's 1934 Oscar-winning comedy, *It Happened One Night*. In that movie, Clark Gable nervously munches on carrots.

Why Does He Say, "What's Up, Doc?" No one knows exactly where this phrase came from, either. In the 1939 screwball comedy *My Man Godfrey*, William Powell uses the line "What's up, Duke?" repeatedly. On the other hand, director Tex Avery had a habit of calling everyone Doc—so he may have inspired the phrase.

IMPRESSIVE STATS

Bugs Bunny is the world's most popular rabbit:

• Since 1939, he has starred in over 175 films.

• He's been nominated for three Oscars, and won one—in 1958, for "Knighty Knight, Bugs."

• In 1985 he became the second cartoon character to be given a star on the Hollywood Walk of Fame (Mickey Mouse was the first).

• For almost 30 years, starting in 1960, he had one of the top-rated shows on Saturday-morning TV.

• In 1976, when researchers polled Americans on their favorite characters, real and imaginary, Bugs came in second…behind Abraham Lincoln.

• More than 1,000 animators worked on Bugs's 1996 movie *Space Jam*, which he starred in with Michael Jordan.

MISNAMED FOOD

Some well-known foods with misleading names.

BUTTERMILK. There's no butter in buttermilk—this thick, sour-tasting drink is made from skim milk treated with bacteria. (*Yech!*)

BOSTON CREAM PIE. It's a cake, not a pie: two layers of white cake with cream filling and chocolate icing.

ENGLISH MUFFIN. It *is* English—they call it a crumpet—but technically, it's not a muffin. A real muffin has no yeast; an English muffin does.

LEMON SOLE. This fish may be delish…but there's no lemon in it. The "lemon" comes from the mistranslation of the French word *limande*, meaning "rough skin."

HEADCHEESE. It's sausage—not cheese—made from a pig's or calf's head, molded with gelatin. (Mmm! Tasty!)

SWEETBREADS. Not a bread and not sweet. It's the pancreas of a young animal, served as a meat. (Extra tasty! *Supersize it!*)

PLUM PUDDING. You can look for them, but you won't find any plums in plum pudding, just candied fruits, raisins, nuts, and spices.

REFRIED BEANS. It sounds like these beans are fried twice, right? Wrong. It's a mistranslation of the Spanish *frijoles refritos*, meaning "well-fried beans."

MNEMONICS

What's a mnemonic (ni-MAH-nik)? It's a device that helps you remember things. Here are some of our favorites.

1. The directions on a compass in clockwise order: North, East, South, West—**N**ever **E**at **S**hredded **W**heat

2. The colors of the spectrum: Red, Orange, Yellow, Green, Blue, Indigo, Violet—**ROYGBIV** (picture a man named **Roy G. Biv**)

3. The four major vocal parts: Soprano, Tenor, Alto, Bass—**STAB**

4. The Great Lakes: Huron, Ontario, Michigan, Erie, Superior—**HOMES**

5. How to set clocks to adjust to daylight saving time: **Spring ahead; fall back**

6. The number of days in the months of the year: **Thirty days hath September, / April, June, and November, / All the rest have thirty-one, / Excepting February alone**

7. The order of the planets from the Sun: **M**ercury, **V**enus, **E**arth, **M**ars, **J**upiter, **S**aturn, **U**ranus, **N**eptune, **P**luto—**M**y **V**ery **E**ducated **M**other **J**ust **S**howed **U**s **N**ine **P**lanets

8. The notes on a treble clef: the lines—**E**very **G**ood **B**oy **D**oes **F**ine; the spaces between the lines—**A**ll **C**ows **E**at **G**rass

TRAILBLAZER

*She was only a kid by today's standards, but
Sacagawea (meaning "bird woman") made
a giant contribution to American history.*

INTO THE WILDERNESS

Have you ever heard of Lewis and Clark? From
1804 to 1806, Meriwether Lewis, William Clark,
and a group of 28 courageous explorers set out to map
the uncharted territory of North America, from the
Missouri River to the Pacific Ocean.

On foot, on horseback, by keelboat, and by canoe,
they traveled 8,000 treacherous miles from Pennsylvania to the Pacific Ocean and then back again.
Although the land was familiar to the Native Americans who lived there, members of the Lewis and Clark
expedition were the first white people to travel it.

GIRL POWER

In the winter of 1804, only five months into their trek,
the explorers took shelter along the Missouri River at
Fort Mandan. It was here that a French Canadian trapper
named Toussaint Charbonneau and his Shoshone wife,
Sacagawea, joined the expedition. Sacagawea was only
15 years old—and she had a baby—but she knew the western land and could speak the Shoshone and Hidatsa languages, so Lewis and Clark hired the family as interpreters.

The following April, the team resumed their trip and

took to the waters of the Missouri River, this time with the help of the Indian girl.

Sacagawea guided the explorers through the heavily forested terrain. When they couldn't hunt game for food, she gathered roots such as licorice and wild artichokes to keep them alive. She found enough food to feed the entire group of 33 people.

DISARMING ELEMENT

As they traveled west, they encountered many new Native American tribes, some of whom had never seen white people before and were suspicious of them. But when they saw Sacagawea, they became friendly—a war party never traveled with a woman (not to mention a baby).

Once the team reached the Rocky Mountains, Sacagawea knew she was close to her native Shoshone home in what is now Idaho. She soon ran into her childhood friend Jumping Fish, who brought the group to the Shoshone camp. There, Sacagawea was reunited with her brothers, one of whom was the tribal chief.

THE JOURNEY CONTINUES

The Shoshone gave Lewis and Clark horses in order to cross the mountains, and the team continued their long journey toward the Pacific. Sacagawea and other members of her tribe continued with them. That winter they reached the coast and stayed at Fort Clatsop, near present-day Astoria, Oregon, until the season passed.

On the journey back east, Sacagawea piloted the

expedition along the Shoshone trails she remembered from her childhood. The most important trail: a road through the mountains known today as Bozeman Pass, Montana.

JOURNEY'S END

Lewis and Clark safely concluded their trip across the continent. In August of 1806, Sacagawea and Charbonneau left them and went to live with the Mandan in South Dakota.

Today Sacagawea is remembered as one of the most important members of the exploration team, yet she was the only one to receive no pay for her services. Although it's uncertain exactly what happened to her after she left the party, historians speculate that Sacagawea died only a few years later, in her mid-twenties.

Follow the route: The Lewis and Clark Expedition began in Pittsburgh, Pennsylvania and went all the way to the Pacific Ocean…and back.

What do you call the plastic or metal tip of a shoelace? An *aglet*.

STILL MORE GROSS STUFF

Essential information about your body and the gooey stuff that comes out of it.

EYE GUNK

After a lovely night's sleep, you wake up in the morning with yellow crusty stuff caked in the inside corner of your eyes. How'd it get there?

All day long, your tear ducts release three kinds of fluid: the salty substance we call tears, an oily liquid that keeps your tears from evaporating, and a layer of mucus that makes the tears stick to your eyeballs.

Every time you blink, your eyelids are like windshield wipers, washing and protecting your eyes. When you're asleep, this liquid keeps flowing, but you don't keep blinking. And if your eyelids aren't quite closed, air gets to this liquid and it dries out. The result: A big hunk of "sand" in your eyes in the morning.

ACNE

Zits, pimples, blackheads, whiteheads—these are the curse of being a teenager. They can make you feel like you have mini-volcanoes on your face.

Zits usually raise their ugly heads around puberty, when your hormones are busy changing your kid body

---

Q: What's an *eructation*?   A: That's what doctors call a burp.

into an adult body. What's happening? The sebaceous (oil) glands in your skin are going wild. These glands keep your skin stretchy and soft as you grow, but sometimes they get a little too active and the oil clogs the sweat glands and hair follicles around them.

As the oil builds up, dead skin cells stick to it. Now you've got a microscopic mountain of crud building up on your face. The plug at the top is white pus, made of white blood cells (which fight bacteria). That's a whitehead. If this oily plug pushes through to the air, it turns dark and becomes—you guessed it—a blackhead. And it's not just your face—pimples can appear anywhere on your body...except the palms of your hands and the bottoms of your feet.

DANDRUFF

Is it snowing? No. When pieces of your scalp flake off and litter the shoulders of your black T-shirt, you've got dandruff. But if you think your head is flaking like that because your scalp is dry, you're wrong.

Your head is shedding pieces of dead skin, and the oil produced by the sebaceous glands in your scalp makes them stick together. So, one of those snowflake-sized flakes is actually thousands of dead skin cells glued together by too much oil. An oily scalp can cause dandruff, but the same things that cause skin rashes can start it, too. And some people get dandruff when they're ill. How do you get rid of dandruff? Shampoo more often. If it's *really* bad, try a dandruff shampoo or see your doctor.

If Earth were the size of an apple, its atmosphere would be thinner than an apple peel.

COLORS

*Here are some more things researchers have
found out about people and colors.*

PINK

• Studies show that people almost always believe pastries from a pink box taste better than from any other color box.

• Men believe pink products do the best job but don't want to be seen buying them. If they think someone's watching, they'll choose something brown or blue.

BROWN

• Researchers say a brown suit is "a symbol of informality that invites people to open up." It's recommended for reporters and counselors.

GRAY

• Your eye processes gray more easily than any other color.

ORANGE

• A quick attention-getter. When used on a product, orange loudly proclaims that the product is for everyone.

PALE BLUE

• Pale blue can actually make people feel cooler.

• Blue inhibits the desire to eat—in fact, researchers say people tend to eat less from blue plates.

• Since blue is associated with eating less, marketers use it to sell products like club soda, skim milk, and cottage cheese.

GREEN

• It's used to sell vegetables and chewing gum but not meat, because it reminds consumers of mold.

Your hair and fingernails grow faster in summer than they do in winter.

MYTHICAL CREATURES

More origins of legendary beasts from mythology.

Creature: Medusa
Where It's From: Greece
Creature's Features: *Medusa* is one of three ugly sisters called the Gorgons. How ugly? One look at Medusa will turn you to stone. Medusa was once a great beauty until she made the goddess Athena angry. Big mistake! Athena changed Medusa into a hideous winged monster with writhing snakes growing out of her head. It was Perseus who figured out a way to destroy Medusa. By looking only at her reflection in his shield, and not directly at her, he got close enough to cut off her head.

Creature: Griffin
Where It's From: Egypt/Assyria (Iraq)
Creature's Features: Tales of the noble *Griffin* first appeared more than 5,000 years ago. It has the head, claws, and wings of an eagle and the hind parts of a lion. It can fly as fast as lightning. Fierce and brave, Griffins often guard great treasures. Some people in the Middle Ages were sure a Griffin guarded the Holy Grail. This is probably why it appears on so many family crests. Gold and Griffins are never far apart. So if you're looking for

---

If you named your cat Tiger, you're not alone—it's the most popular cat name in the U.S.

gold, check out the Griffin's nest, which is said to be lined with that precious metal.

Creature: Minotaur
Where It's From: Crete, Greece
Creature's Features: The *Minotaur* was a real bully! His mother was Queen Pasiphae, and his father was a bull, so he had the head of a bull and the body of a man. His stepfather, King Minos, was so disgusted by the horrible creature that he imprisoned the Minotaur in the Labyrinth—a maze so complicated that no one could ever find a way out. Each year, 14 young men and women were forced into the maze to satisfy the Minotaur's appetite. But a clever prince named Theseus unwound a spool of thread as he made his way to the heart of the Labyrinth. There, he killed the Minotaur, then followed the trail of thread back to safety.

Creature: Cerberus
Where It's From: Greece
Creature's Features: *Cerberus* is no ordinary guard dog. For one thing, this puppy has three heads. For another, he's no puppy, he's as big as a house. And stay away from his tail—it's a snake. You'll find Cerberus guarding the gates of Hell. Actually, they're gates of Persephone's palace in Hades. Persephone is the Queen of the Underworld. This "super-Doberman" doesn't just look after Persephone, though—he's got his eye on all the souls who enter Hades. His bark tells them when to come in, and his bite snags them if they try to get out.

A FOOD IS BORN

Here are some more origins of common food brands.

HAWAIIAN PUNCH

It wasn't invented in Hawaii…and it wasn't invented by Hawaiians. It was actually invented in 1936 by two Californians, A. W. Leo and Tom Yates. "It began as a soda fountain syrup," writes Vince Staten in *Can You Trust a Tomato in January?* "Mixed with water it was a drink, but was also used as an ice cream topping." In the 1940s, department stores sold the syrup in their gourmet food sections. And a few years later, Leo put it into a pre-mixed 46-ounce bottle. But it didn't become really popular until the early 1960s, when the company ran TV commercials featuring a cartoon character in a Hawaiian shirt offering a friend "a nice Hawaiian Punch" and then socking him in the nose.

WHEATIES

Invented in 1921 by a health spa owner who fed his patients homemade bran gruel to help them lose weight. One day he spilled some of the gruel on the stove, and it hardened into a crust. About to throw it out, he decided to eat it instead. The flakes he scraped off tasted better than the stuff in the pot…so he made more and showed them to a friend at the Washburn Crosby Company. People there liked the flakes but didn't like how they crumbled. So they made a better flake using wheat and held a contest to name the product. The winner: Wheaties.

NASA invented the Dustbuster.

MYTH AMERICA

Here are some patriotic stories we learned when we were young... all of which are 100% baloney.

THE MYTH: The framers of the U.S. Constitution saw it for the great document that it was.

THE TRUTH: A lot of the delegates at the Constitutional Convention hated it. So many compromises had to be made that many participants viewed it as, in Alexander Hamilton's words, "weak and worthless." Fifteen delegates refused to sign it, and even the Constitution's biggest supporters saw it as little more than a temporary solution—delegates thought that after a few years passed they would meet at a new convention and try to pass something better. But, of course, they never did.

THE MYTH: Representatives from the 13 colonies met in Philadelphia in 1787 and drafted the U.S. Constitution.

THE TRUTH: Rhode Island didn't send delegates. And Maryland almost didn't, because officials had a hard time finding anyone willing to go. The first five people they asked refused, and the state was still looking for people to send when the Constitutional Convention opened. New Hampshire was willing to send delegates but unwilling to pay expenses, so they went for weeks without representation. "Many delegates attended only occasionally, and six never came at all,"

If you had a million $1 bills (you wish!), they'd weigh about 2,040 pounds.

Bill Bryson writes in *Made in America*. "Only 30 of the 61 elected delegates attended from start to finish."

THE MYTH: The Founding Fathers believed in democracy.

THE TRUTH: "The men who framed the Constitution disagreed about many things," writes Paul Boller in *Not So!*, "but on one point they were in complete agreement: democracy meant mob rule and unchecked, it would pose a grave threat to life, liberty and property....There was nothing unusual in their distrust of democracy; it was conventional wisdom in the 18th century. Even well into the 19th century, in the U.S. as well as Western Europe, the word 'democracy' had an unsavory connotation."

THE MYTH: The United States came very close to making German the official language of the country.

THE TRUTH: History books occasionally report that German missed becoming our language by one vote in the Continental Congress. The reason they give: Colonists wanted to put as much distance between themselves and England as possible. Actually, dumping English was never considered. By 1790, 90% of the white population of the United States was of English descent.

"The only known occasion on which German was ever an issue was in 1795," Bryson writes, "when the House of Representatives considered a proposal to publish federal laws in German as well as in English as a convenience to recent immigrants. The proposal was defeated."

AMAZING L🜉CK

Dumb luck—sometimes we're blessed with it, sometimes we're cursed with it. Here are some examples of people who lucked out.

CELLULAR MEMORY

"In the Dent de Crolles region in France, shepherd Christian Raymond, 23, was rescued from a cliff from which he had been hanging by his fingers. He had called the emergency rescue operator on his cell phone earlier in the day and managed to make another call from the cliff by pressing 'redial' with his nose against the phone, which had fallen down the mountain with him but had landed right beside him."

—"The Edge," *The Oregonian*

MY FORTUNE FOR A KISS

"Hauled before a Melbourne court in 1907 for hugging and kissing the elderly Hazel Moore when she entered his shop, young Michael O'Connor defended himself by claiming it had been a lovely spring day and he was in high spirits. O'Connor had to serve a few months for breach of peace. So imagine his amazement 10 years later when an attorney representing Miss Moore's estate gave him 20,000 pounds (about $10,000)! She left the fortune in memory of the only kiss she had received from a man in her adult life."

—*Oops!*

WAVES OF JOY

"In December 1948, Navy Lieutenant (and future U.S. president) Jimmy Carter was on night duty on the bridge of his submarine, the USS *Pomfret*, which was riding on the surface, recharging its batteries. Suddenly, an enormous wave crashed across the sub and over Carter's head. Unable to keep his hold on the railing, Carter found himself swimming inside the wave with no sense of what was up or down.

By pure chance, the wave set Carter down on the submarine's gun turret thirty feet from the bridge. He felt he was watched over by God, and said, 'I don't have any fear at all of death.'"

—*Oh Say Can You See*

AMAZING LOTTERY WINNERS

• "Randy Halvorson was one of 14 employees to share a $3.4 million jackpot in 1988. The Iowa resident then won $7.2 million with his brother in 1990."

• "In Wisconsin, Donald Smith of Amherst has won the state's SuperCash game three times: On May 25, 1993, June 17, 1994, and July 30, 1995. He won $250,000 each time. The odds of winning the Super-Cash game just once are nearly one in a million."

• "Joseph P. Crowley won $3 million in the Ohio lottery in 1987. Six years later, he retired to Boca Raton, Florida, and played the Florida Lotto on Christmas Day of 1993. He won $20 million."

—*The Good Luck Book*

BODY MUSIC: THE HICCUP

Your body is a fine musical instrument, making sounds that entertain (and gross out) your friends and family.

HIC!
You've been running. You down a glass of soda pop. Your diaphragm suddenly contracts and…*hic!* You've got the hiccups. This can happen when you drink or eat too fast. It can happen if you are excited or scared. It can happen if you have an irritation in your stomach or throat. But believe it or not, nobody really knows *why* it happens.

HIC!

We do know that when you hiccup, your diaphragm contracts. Your diaphragm, by the way, is a dome-shaped muscle that stretches across your chest below your lungs. It's the muscle that goes in and out when you breathe. When the diaphragm suddenly contracts, or "flinches," it causes your vocal cords to slam shut. And that's what makes the "hic" sound.

AND THE WINNER IS…HIC!

Most hiccups stop after a few minutes. But for some people, hiccups can last for months or even years (they're called *intractable* hiccups). The world-record

A *chortle* is the noise you make when you chuckle and snort at the same time.

holder for most hiccups goes to an American pig farmer who hiccuped from 1922 to 1987. That's 65 years!

HIC! HELP! HIC!

Everyone has a surefire cure for the hiccups. But in case you don't, here are a few you might want to try (don't blame us if they don't work!):

• Swallow a spoonful of sugar every two minutes. Repeat three times.

• Heimlich hiccups: Place the fingers of both hands together right below the center of your rib cage. Gently press in and up at the same time. It's the same spot that's pushed in the Heimlich maneuver, but you don't need to use force—just a little pressure on that spot, and your hiccups could be history!

• Hold your breath for as long as possible.

• Drink water quickly.

• Drink water from the wrong side of the glass. (*No spilling.*)

• Breathe in and out of a paper bag.

• Eat crushed ice.

• Eat ginger.

• Eat a tablespoon of peanut butter.

• Cover each ear with your fingers and press gently for a few minutes.

• Pull your hair from the top of your head for a minute.

• And the old tried-and-true: have somebody scare the daylights out of you!

Q: What's a *singultus?*   A: That's what doctors call a hiccup.

THE NOSE KNOWS

Smell is an amazing and complex function carried out in a tiny chamber, half the size of an egg, situated just behind our noses. With it, we are able to smell thousands of different odors.

THE SCIENCE OF SMELL

How do we smell things? Scientists tell us the air is filled with "odor molecules." They enter your nasal cavity (the space right inside your nose) every time you breathe—23,000 times a day.

• Just behind your nose, these molecules are absorbed by mucus-covered tissue.

• This tissue is covered with "receptor" cells. (You have millions of them.) Each receptor cell is mounted on a microscopic hair.

• The receptor cells stick out and wave in the air currents we inhale. At least 40 of them have to detect odor molecules before a smell is registered.

• When a new smell is detected, the tiny *olfactory bulb*, located just above the nasal cavity, flashes data directly to the most ancient and mysterious part of your brain— the limbic system—which handles feelings and instincts. The limbic system reacts immediately, before the rest of your brain can think about it, and may provoke powerful emotions or images. (If you've ever smelled something that instantly brought back a memory, like maybe suntan lotion reminding you of summer, that was your limbic system in action.)

There are more Barbie dolls in Italy than there are Canadians in Canada.

THE DARK AGES OF SMELLING

Today, a keen sense of smell is considered a good thing to have—but it wasn't always appreciated.

• The ancient philosopher Plato looked down on smell as a lowly instinct that might lead to gluttony and lust, while vision and hearing opened one to geometry and music and were therefore "closer to the soul."

• During the 18th and 19th centuries, it was commonly believed that many diseases were caused by smells. Odors from corpses, feces, urine, swamps, and the Earth were called *miasmas* and were thought to have the power to kill people. To ward off these smells, people carried and inhaled *antimephitics*, such as garlic, amber, sulfur, and incense. When exposed to miasmic odors, people were careful not to swallow their saliva, but spat it out instead. The Viennese physician Semmelweis was ridiculed by colleagues when he declared that washing one's hands, not breathing antimephitics, would stop most diseases from spreading.

• According to some sources, the stethoscope was invented not to hear heartbeats better, but to give doctors some distance from a patient's body odors.

SMELL AND TASTE

• Our sense of taste is limited to sweet, sour, salt, and

bitter. It's the smells that make us really taste. For example, cheese's smell, not its taste, is what makes it delicious. With a head cold, eating cheese is an entirely different experience.

• Scientists have categorized smells into seven groups: minty like peppermint, floral like roses, ethereal like pears, musky like—well—musk, resinous like mothballs, foul like rotten eggs, and acrid like vinegar.

• Talking with your mouth full expels taste molecules and diminishes the taste of food.

SMELLY FACTS

• Women have a keener sense of smell than men.

• By simply smelling a piece of clothing, most people can tell if it was worn by a woman or man.

• Each of us has an odor that is, like our fingerprints, unique. One result of this, say researchers: Some of the thrill of kissing someone comes from smelling the unique odors of their face.

• Smells stimulate learning. Students given olfactory stimulation (in other words, a smell) along with a word list retain much more information and remember it longer.

• Many smells are heavier than air and can be smelled only at ground level.

• We smell scents best if we take several short sniffs, rather than one long one.

ASK THE EXPERTS

Here are some more head-scratching questions,
with answers from top trivia experts.

G **ET A LEG UP**
Q: *Do centipedes really have 100 legs?*
A: "The house centipede (the kind you're most likely to see under your refrigerator) can have as few as 30 legs or, for really big specimens, more than 350. All those legs enable them to move with incredible speed: One was clocked at an incredible 17 inches per second.

"Although most people don't like to share their home with centipedes, they can be quite helpful. They're not dangerous, and they eat flies and cockroaches." (From *101 Questions and Answers About Backyard Wildlife*, by Ann Squire)

IN THE MIDNIGHT HOUR

Q: *Which is correct: 12 midnight a.m. or p.m.?*
A: "Neither. That's because midnight doesn't belong either to the day before or the day after. Midnight is the dividing line between days, just as the present is the dividing line between the future and the past. So it's 12 midnight, period.

"Twelve noon works the same way—it's neither a.m. nor p.m. Just 12 noon, period." (From *Know It All!*, by Ed Zotti)

The average eyelash lasts 150 days before it falls out and a new one takes its place.

CELEBRITY SECRETS

*Here's the BRI's tabloid section—a bunch
of gossip about famous people.*

ALBERT EINSTEIN

Claim to Fame: Nobel Prize-winning physicist
• As a boy, he applied to the Federal Polytechnic Academy in Zürich, Switzerland, but flunked the entrance exam. When his father asked the headmaster what profession Albert should adopt, he was told, "It doesn't matter, he'll never amount to anything."

• For many years, Einstein thought of his work in physics as a hobby. He regarded himself as a failure...because he really wanted to be a concert violinist.

MUHAMMAD ALI

Claim to Fame: World-champion heavyweight boxer
• For some reason, as a child, he always walked on his tiptoes. When he got older, he played touch football, but wouldn't play tackle because he thought it was too rough.

Albert Einstein slept 10 hours a night.

• Because he was afraid to fly, he almost didn't make it to the 1960 Rome Olympics, where he won the gold medal that launched his career.

MICHAEL JACKSON

Claim to Fame: Singer, self-proclaimed "King of Pop"

• Jackson's favorite song? "My Favorite Things," performed by Julie Andrews.

• His opinion of other singers: Paul McCartney? Okay writer, not much of an entertainer. "I do better box office than he does." Frank Sinatra? "I don't know what people see in the guy. He's a legend, but he wasn't much of a singer." Mick Jagger? "He sings flat. How did he ever get to be a star? I just don't get it." Madonna? "She just isn't that good....She can't sing. She's just an OK dancer.... She knows how to market herself. That's about it."

WILLIAM SHATNER

Claim to Fame: *Star Trek*'s Captain Kirk

• Swears he's seen a UFO. "You'd almost think he was joking," writes Tim Harrower in the Portland *Oregonian*, "but, no, Shatner was serious when he reported that a silver spacecraft flew over him in the Mojave Desert as he pushed his inoperative motorcycle. He also claims to have received a telepathic message from the beings in the craft advising him which direction to walk."

*   *   *

"Let us be thankful for fools. If not for them the rest of us could not succeed."

—**Mark Twain**

The image on the back of a U.S. coin is always upside down compared to the front.

LUCKY SPORTS

Some people carry a rabbit's foot for luck—which is kind of funny, because it's not very lucky for the rabbit. Here are some wacky superstitions from the world of sports.

Race car driver **Christian Fittipaldi** is one of the best when it comes to driving in the rain, so he wants it to rain every race. Good luck charm: His million-dollar race car has a rubber ducky attached to the hood.

Basketball great **Michael Jordan** played college ball for the North Carolina Tarheels. As a pro, he always wore his blue Tarheel shorts under his uniform for good luck.

"The goal posts are my friends," says hockey goalie **Patrick Roy**. So he has pregame "chats" with the posts. When asked if they talk back, he said, "Yes. The say 'PING!'"

Olympic speed skater **Bonnie Blair** ate a peanut butter and jelly sandwich before every race. Did it work? She won five gold medals.

NFL head coach **George Seifert** won the Super Bowl twice. His superstitions: He wears his lucky blue sweater every Monday; eats Chinese food every Tuesday; refuses to step on the helmet painted on the practice field; and before every game, runs a ritual lap around the locker room without his shirt on.

Hard to imagine: In 1910, Georgia Tech's football team beat Cumberland University 222 to 0.

A CLASSIC HOAX

Here's one of our favorite stories—about an amazing prank that was pulled just to see if the pranksters could get away with it. (And, by the way…it's a true story.)

THE MANHATTAN ISLAND HOAX
Background: In 1824 a New Yorker remembered today only by his last name—Lozier—stood up on a soapbox in Manhattan's busy Centre Market and announced to the crowd that because of all the buildings recently constructed, the southern tip of Manhattan Island had become too heavy and was in danger of sinking. The solution, he said, was to saw the island off at the northern end, tow it out to sea, turn it 180 degrees around, and reattach it.

Lozier claimed that sawing Manhattan Island in half would be one of the biggest public works projects New York had ever seen, and that Mayor Stephen Allen had put him in charge of the project.

The idea sounded preposterous to most of Lozier's listeners, but then again, so had the idea of building the Erie Canal (the large canal that created a new shipping route, connecting the Hudson River to Lake Erie), and that wonder of the world was nearly finished. Besides, if it wasn't true, why would Lozier say publicly that the mayor had authorized him to handle the project?

What Happened: Well, Lozier must have been a persuasive speaker, because a lot of people believed him.

Deer like to play tag. They tag each other using their hooves.

He began signing up hundreds of laborers to work on the project, offering triple wages to anyone willing to saw underwater. He directed blacksmiths and carpenters to begin designing the 100-foot saws and 250-foot oars needed to saw the island off and row it out to sea. He also arranged for the construction of barracks and mess halls for his laborers, and the delivery of 500 cattle, 500 hogs, and 3,000 chickens, so his workers would have plenty to eat.

After two months of planning, the date arrived for construction to begin. Scores of laborers, carpenters, blacksmiths, butchers, and animals—as well as a marching band and hundreds of onlookers—arrived at Spring Street and Bowery to see the historic project get underway. About the only people who didn't show up were Lozier and his accomplices, who'd suddenly left town "on account of their health."

They were actually holed up in Brooklyn, and although there was talk of having them arrested, no one really wanted to make a formal complaint to the authorities. Why? Nobody wanted to admit they'd been fooled…so Lozier got away scot-free.

PALINDROMES

Palindromes are words or sentences that are spelled the same way backward or forward. Here are some of our favorites.

A dog! A panic in a pagoda!

I'm a boob, am I?

Dog doo! Good god!

"Do orbits all last?" I brood.

Emil, a sleepy baby, peels a lime.

Party boobytrap.

He spots one last sale. No stops, eh?

Neil. An alien.

Go hang a salami! I'm a lasagna hog!

Madame, not one man is selfless; I name not one, Madam.

Ma is a nun, as I am.

So, Ed, I vow to do two videos.

Yo! Bozo boy!

Wonton? Not now.

Cigar? Toss it in a can, it is so tragic.

Diana saw I was an aid.

Stella wondered: "No wallets?"

Ron, I'm a minor.

So, Ida, adios!

A Toyota! Race fast, safe car. A Toyota.

Doc, note, I dissent. A fast never prevents a fatness. I diet on cod.

Sit on a potato pan, Otis!

Four things that kill germs: 1) Sunshine; 2) Fresh air; 3) Soapy water; 4) Tears.

TOMATO FACTS

Here are some interesting facts about
tomatoes from the BRI files.

THE TOMATO ARRIVES

• The first tomato plants grew wild in Peru. They weren't much like today's tomato—they were small. Over time, naturally-occurring mutations made them closer to what we eat today. The mutated tomatoes were cultivated by native Central American farmers. Spanish explorers "discovered" them there and brought them to Europe.

• In 1597 English physician John Gerard wrote that tomatoes were poisonous—even though he knew they were eaten in Spain and Italy—and people believed him. Result: Until the 1700s, most English people were afraid to eat tomatoes.

A CULTIVATED TASTE

• Legend has it that Thomas Jefferson was the first person to cultivate tomatoes in America, but that's just a myth. Though he was an early advocate of the tomato in America—he was growing them at his estate by 1809—he didn't introduce them; they were already here. The rumor probably started because Jefferson loved to serve tomatoes to guests—many of whom tasted them for the first time at his home.

Highest flying bird: the bar-headed goose—it can go as high as 30,000 feet.

• In 1834 a book by an American doctor named John Bennet claimed tomatoes were good for you. It caught the public's fancy and tomatoes were suddenly "in."

• In 1837 someone invented "tomato pills." A massive ad campaign for the pills brought tomatoes to the public's attention like never before: cookbooks, newspapers, and magazines all raved about the wonder fruit. Doctors actually prescribed them as medicine.

• Tomatomania died down over the next decade, but by then tomatoes were widely popular and could be found in farms, gardens—and on dining tables—all across America.

• By 1870 tomatoes ranked among the top three vegetables, along with peas and corn.

RANDOM TOMATO BITS

• Settlers in Oregon ate their tomatoes pulverized into a thick paste that they smeared over hotcakes.

• In 1984 NASA sent 12.5 million tomato seeds into space for six years. Later, the seeds were given to schoolteachers across the country to grow in their classrooms. Uproar over possible mutations led NASA to recommend that students not eat the tomatoes.

• The world's biggest tomato, according to the *Guinness Book of World Records*, was grown in 1986 by Gordon Graham and weighed in at nearly eight pounds.

• During the 19th century the tomato was called a "love apple."

JABBERWOCKY

Here's one of Uncle John's favorite poems (he learned it in fifth grade). Written by Lewis Carroll, the author of Alice's Adventures in Wonderland, *it's a tale about conquering the unknown. It may sound like nonsense... but is it really?*

'Twas brillig, and the slithy toves
Did gyre and gimble in the wabe;
All mimsy were the borogoves,
And the mome raths outgrabe.

"Beware the Jabberwock, my son!
The jaws that bite, the claws that catch!
Beware the Jubjub bird, and shun
The frumious Bandersnatch!"

He took his vorpal sword in hand:
Long time the manxome for he sought—
So rested he by the Tumtum tree,
And stood awhile in thought.

According to recent estimates, 99% of the universe is nothing.

And as in uffish thought he stood,
The Jabberwock, with eyes of flame,
Came whiffling through the tulgey wood,
And burbled as it came!

One, two! One, two!
And through and through
The vorpal blade went snicker-snack!
He left it dead, and with its head
He went galumphing back.

"And hast thou slain the Jabberwock?
Come to my arms, my beamish boy!
O frabjous day! Callooh! Callay!"
He chortled in his joy.

'Twas brillig, and the slithy toves
Did gyre and gimble in the wabe;
All mimsy were the borogoves,
And the mome raths outgrabe.

YUCKY QUIZ

Here's a chance to gross yourself out and have fun at the same time.

1) How many sweat glands does your body have?
a. Thousands **b.** Millions **c.** Billions

2) Which of these body parts has no sweat glands?
a. Your belly button **b.** Your lips **c.** Your ears

3) How many bacteria are in your colon, the final stop in the digestive system before solid waste is dumped?
a. Thousands **b.** Millions **c.** Billions

4) At about 6 lbs., what is your body's heaviest organ?
a. Your skin **b.** Your liver **c.** Your heart

5) What's the fastest a sneeze can fly out of your mouth?
a. 106 mph **b.** 53 mph **c.** 13 mph

6) What part of your body has the most sweat glands?
a. Your feet **b.** Your butt **c.** Your armpits

7) If you don't brush your teeth for a few days, how many bacteria might soon be living on just one tooth?
a. A billion **b.** A thousand **c.** None

8) What happens when bacteria gets trapped in one of your skin pores?
a. They scream **b.** You get a zit **c.** Your skin dries out

Answers:

1. b; 2. b; 3. c; 4. a; 5. a; 6. a; 7. a; 8. b

An elephant's heart beats about 25 times a minute. A mouse's, about 650 times.

READ ALL ABOUT IT!

Two good reasons not to believe everything you read in the newspapers.

THE STORY: In the early 1920s, the *Toronto Mail and Empire* reported that two scientists named Dr. Schmierkase and Dr. Butterbrod had discovered "what appeared to be the fossil of the whale that had swallowed Jonah."

The next day, preachers all over Toronto read the story from the pulpit, citing it as proof that the biblical story of Jonah was true.

THE TRUTH: Three days later, the *Toronto Mail and Empire* ran a second story exposing the first one as a hoax, the work of a journalist named Charles Langdon Clarke.

Clarke liked to make up news items based on biblical stories and then attribute them to fictional newspapers like the *Babylon Gazette* or *Jerusalem Times*. Anyone who spoke German could have guessed the story was a joke—Dr. Schmierkase and Dr. Butterbrod translates to Dr. Cheese and Dr. Butterbread.

THE STORY: In 1987 the *San Diego Metropolitan* claimed that the Great American Bank Building, one of San Diego's best-known landmarks, was haunted.

Q: What's the difference between a hare and a rabbit?

Creepy voices and mysterious footsteps were heard late at night; ghostlike images were seen materializing out of thin air. The article also claimed that the ghost was helping the building's janitors do the vacuuming. The article even included a "photo" of the ghost.

THE TRUTH: The article was a hoax, the brainchild of *Metropolitan* publisher Sean Patrick Reily. Reily admitted that he had concocted the phony story, but not before tenants of the Great American Bank Building read about the incidents and began reporting their own "sightings"— including power failures, carpeting that had been "mysteriously vacuumed," and cleaning equipment that moved from one floor to another. (One electrician even reported seeing his tools float in midair.)

*   *   *

POP QUIZ

Which soft drink was invented at The Old Corner Drug Store in Waco, Texas, in 1885?

Answer:

Dr Pepper

TRAVEL GUIDE TO IMAGINARY LANDS

Let Uncle John be your guide to some fantastic places that can only be found in books. Forget the movies—there's nothing like a great novel.

MIDDLE EARTH

Where You'll Find It: J. R. R. Tolkien's *The Lord of the Rings*

Adventure Awaits You: From the green gardens of the Shire to darkest depths of Mordor, you'll be traveling with friendly hobbits, mystical elves, and a wise wizard. Your quest: destroy the Ring and save Middle Earth.

But Beware: There's magic in the land, and not all of it is good. You'll encounter evil orcs, ancient dragons, and trolls. Scared? You should be. But remain brave and true to your quest…and you'll never be alone.

NARNIA

Where You'll Find It: C. S. Lewis's *The Chronicles of Narnia*

Adventure Awaits You: Think a closet is just a closet? It's much more than that for Peter, Susan, Edmund, and Lucy—four kids who find a magic portal to an enchanted world where animals talk and adventure abounds.

But Beware: You must help save Narnia from Jadis the White Witch. To aid you in your quest is Aslan, a giant lion with massive strength and infinite wisdom. There are many more creatures to discover, too, from unicorns and marsh-wiggles to mermaids and wood spirits.

NEVER-NEVER LAND

Where You'll Find It: J. M. Barrie's *Peter Pan*

Adventure Awaits You: Children on the edge of sleep can sometimes travel to Never-Never Land. Or you may get sprinkled with fairy dust and fly there with Peter Pan himself. Need directions? "Take the second star to the right and head straight on 'til morning."

But Beware: There's a nasty bunch of pirates in Never-Never Land, led by the fiendish Captain Hook. And he doesn't like little children! It's up to you, the Lost Boys, Tinkerbell, and Peter Pan to stop him. But always listen for the tick…tick…tick of the hungry ticking crocodile.

OZ

Where You'll Find It: L. Frank Baum's *The Wonderful Wizard of Oz*

Adventure Awaits You: Getting to Oz isn't easy: Dorothy Gale had to bump her head and be swept away inside a tornado. But all you need to do is turn the book's pages to enter this strange world where there is no money, no sickness, and no poverty. The streets are paved with emeralds. And inside the gated walls of the Emerald City are fantastical houses and odd creatures…not to mention a mysterious wizard.

But Beware: The Wicked Witch of the West doesn't want you there, and she'll do anything to stop you and your friends—and that little dog, too. Watch out for poison poppies, flying monkeys, and fire, fire, fire!

HOGWARTS SCHOOL OF WITCHES AND WIZARDRY

Where You'll Find It: J. K. Rowling's *Harry Potter* series

Adventure Awaits You: Catch the Hogwarts Express on Platform $9^3/_4$ at the King's Crossing train station. Once there, you'll learn how concoct magic spells, fly on a broom, and tame mythical beasts.

But Beware: Not all is as it seems. There is a dark presence from the past trying to crack the foundation of this great school. With the aid of your friends Ron and Hermione, a giant named Hagrid, and a secret helper, you have all of the powers you need to save Hogwarts.

LILLIPUT

Where You'll Find It: Jonathan Swift's *Gulliver's Travels*

Adventure Awaits You: Do you often feel like you're a lot shorter than everyone else? How would you like to visit the island of Lilliput, where the inhabitants are only six inches tall? Join Dr. Lemuel Gulliver as he tells tall tales about a tiny land with tiny inhabitants. Even the horses are tiny—only four and a half inches high.

But Beware: The tiny parents on Lilliput are silly and have silly arguments. They're not even to be trusted raising their own children—kids have to live in public nurseries until they reach the age of 20 moons. And please heed the Lilliputian's warning: While you're there, don't uproot any trees or step on any towns.

Americans spend six times more money on video games than on school supplies.

BEWARE: HAUNTED HOUSE

*A few more stories of ghosts and things that
go bump in the night. Mooo-haaa-haaa.*

HAUNTED HOUSE: Toys R Us
GHOST STORY: A ghost in a toy store? No
way. That's what people used to say until they
visited the Toys R Us store in Sunnyvale, California.
This ghost must like to have fun.

It's not unusual for employees to unlock the doors in
the morning and find toys and books scattered all over
the store. Sometimes objects fly through the air. Workers report being touched when no one is around and
that aisle 15C sometimes smells of fresh flowers. Others
have heard an unfamiliar voice call their name.

Many people have reported ghostly activity in the
women's bathroom, too. The water faucets gush on
when no one is there. If they're turned off, they come
right back on again. Some women report being tapped
on the shoulder. Those with long hair sometimes feel it
being stroked by an unseen hand. Makes you wonder
who it could be. Casper? Why not visit and find out?

HAUNTED HOUSE: The Martha Washington Inn
in Virginia

Q: What do basketball and ice hockey have in common?   A: Both were invented by Canadians.

GHOST STORY: The Inn was used as a hospital during the Civil War. That's when the house picked up more than its share of ghostly guests. On a moonless night you may see a phantom horse outside the front steps. He's waiting patiently for his master, a Union officer who was shot in front of the house.

And there's the matter of the bloodstains on the floorboards outside the Governor's Room. A confederate soldier was shot and killed on that spot as he ran to warn of invading Union soldiers. According to the bellhop, any carpet set down on that spot will get holes in it just above the bloodstains.

The saddest ghost is that of a young nurse named Beth. She fell in love with John Stoves, the soldier she tended in Room 403. To ease his pain as he lay dying, she played the violin. She, herself, died of a fever only a few weeks later. Now her ghost visits his room, and the sad sound of her violin can be heard through the Inn.

HAUNTED HOUSE: Drury Lane Theatre, London
GHOST STORY: If you go to see a play at the Drury Lane Theatre, be sure to save a seat for "The Man in Gray." He wears a long gray coat, a tricornered hat, powdered wig, and sword. He likes to watch the plays from the balcony, where he walks slowly from one end to the other, only to disappear into the wall. There's another ghost who, it's said, often "helps" young actresses along in their performances by guiding them around the stage. He even gives them a little pat on the back when they've done a good job.

Afraid of ghosts? If so, then you have *phasmophobia*.

A FOOD IS BORN

Here are some more origins of classic food favorites.

CHEX CEREALS

When William Danforth was a child, a classmate's mother made clothes for her family from gingham cloth. The odd, checkered clothing made a lasting impression on the townsfolk. That's why, when Danforth wanted a distinctive trademark for his Ralston Purina products, he chose a checkerboard pattern. He became so obsessed with it that he wore red-check ties, jackets, and socks to work...and he even changed the company's address to Checkerboard Square. In 1937 he commissioned a checkerboard breakfast cereal and called it Wheat Chex.

KOOL-AID

In the 1920s, Edwin E. Perkins was president of a company called Onor-Maid that sold more than 125 household products, including spices, food flavorings, and medicines. One of his products was Fruit Smack, an inexpensive, fruit-flavored soft-drink syrup that was popular with people who couldn't afford Coca-Cola. At first, Fruit Smack was shipped in glass bottles, but these were expensive and frequently broke. When Perkins saw how successful the new powdered product called Jell-O was becoming, he decided to sell his syrup in powder form. He renamed it Kool-Aid.

Four most common last names in the U.S.: 1) Smith 2) Johnson 3) Williams 4) Jones.

THE STORY OF LITTLE LEAGUE

*Today the Little League is an American tradition,
but it only came about because someone kept
a promise he made…to himself.*

ACCIDENT OF FATE

It started one afternoon in 1938. A man named Carl Stotz went out into his Williamsport, Pennsylvania, yard to play catch with his two nephews. They wanted to play baseball, but the yard was too small. So they just had a game of catch.

On one throw, a nephew tossed the ball so far that Stotz had to run into the neighbor's yard. He recalled years later, "As I stretched to catch the ball, I stepped into the cutoff stems of a lilac bush that were sticking up several inches above the ground. A sharp stub tore through my sock and scraped my ankle. The pain was intense."

GOOD OL' DAYS

As Stotz sat nursing his ankle, he suddenly remembered that he had played on the same kind of rough ground when he was a kid…and he remembered a promise he'd made to himself when he was a young boy.

Back then, equipment was scarce—he and his friends hit balls with sticks because they didn't have bats. They used baseballs until the skins came off, and then patched them up with tape and used them until there wasn't anything left to tape back together. Some of his friends had even played barefoot because they didn't have any shoes.

"I remembered thinking to myself, 'When I grow up, I'm gonna have a baseball team for boys, complete with uniforms and equipment. They'll play on a real field like the big guys, with cheering crowds at every game.'"

Right then and there, Stotz decided to keep his boyhood promise.

DOWNSIZING THE GAME

He spent the next few months organizing teams and rounding up sponsors to pay for the equipment. At the same time, he set about "shrinking" the game of baseball so 9- to 12-year-old kids could really play.

Stotz found child-sized bats and equipment for his teams, and at every team practice he experimented until he found the ideal size for a field. About the only thing Stotz didn't change was the size of the baseball itself. He wanted kids to be able to practice with any baseball they already had on hand.

"Remember, this was 1938, and the Great Depression was still with many families," he wrote in his autobiography. "I was afraid the expense of buying special balls would be too much for some families and might keep boys from becoming Little Leaguers."

Ha Ha!   Q: Why did the chicken cross the playground?   A: To get to the other slide.

BATTER UP

Stotz finally set the date of the first game: June 6, 1939. But what was the new league going to be called? He'd considered calling it Junior League Baseball or the Little Boys' League, but he couldn't decide. So he let the sports editor of the local Williamsport newspaper choose…and he picked Little League.

Little League grew slowly over the next several years, but by the end of 1950, there were more than 700 local leagues all over the United States. There was even one in British Columbia, Canada—the first outside the U.S.

By 2000, there were more than 7,300 leagues in 102 countries. And in case you're wondering, that's 2,845,425 kids, all playing the game that Carl Stotz started with a dream—Little League baseball.

LITTLE LEAGUE FACTS

• Originally, Little League was for boys only. In 1974 the rules were changed to allow girls to play, too.

• The first team to win the Little League World Series was the Maynard Midgets from Williamsport, Pa., in 1947.

• In the big leagues, the distance from home plate to first base is 90 feet. In Little League, it's 60 feet.

• The Little League Pledge: "I trust in God. / I love my country and will respect its laws. / I will play fair and strive to win. / But win or lose I will always do my best."

• The game of tee ball was invented in 1960 in Bagdad, Florida, by Dayton Hobbs.

ODD WORLD RECORDS

More strange achievements.

F **red Jipp,** New York City
Record: Most illegal marriages. Between 1949 and 1981, using over 50 aliases, he married 104 women in 27 states and 14 foreign countries. He was sentenced to 34 years in prison and fined $336,000.

Nine employees of the Bruntsfield Bedding Centre, Scotland
Record: Pushed a wheeled hospital bed 3,233 miles between June 21 and July 26, 1979.

N. Ravi, Tamil Nadu, India
Record: Stood on one foot for 34 hours in 1982.

Octavio Guillen and Adriana Martinez, Mexico City
Record: Longest engagement: 67 years. They finally got married in 1969. Both were age 82.

"Hercules" John Massis, Oostakker, Belgium
Record: Used his teeth to stop a helicopter from taking off in 1979.

Michel Lotito, Grenoble, France
Record: Has been eating metal and glass since 1959. He has eaten 10 bicycles, a supermarket food cart, 7 televisions, 6 chandeliers, 1 coffin, and 1 Cessna airplane. (Don't try this at home!)

THE TRUTH ABOUT CHRISTOPHER COLUMBUS

The most common myth about Christopher Columbus is that he discovered America. Well, he didn't discover it—there were people here for thousands of years before 1492. And hey, he didn't even land here. He landed on the Caribbean island now known as the Dominican Republic. Here are a few more myths about Columbus.

MYTH #1: Columbus was born in Genoa, Italy. **THE TRUTH:** According to his son Fernando, Columbus never revealed where he was born; he preferred to call himself "a man of the sea." Meanwhile, dozens of places claim to be Columbus's birthplace, including:

• **Corsica.** The town of Calvi claims both his birth and his grave; Columbus has a tombstone there.

• **England.** A book published in 1682 in London states that Columbus was "born in England, but lived in Genoa."

• **France, Spain, Armenia, Poland, and even Norway.** Norwegians say his real name was Christopher Bonde.

MYTH #2: Columbus's boats were officially named

the *Niña*, the *Pinta*, and the *Santa María*.

THE TRUTH: In Columbus's time, if a ship had any kind of name at all, it was unofficial—usually something that the crew came up with. This was true of Columbus's ships as well:

• The *Pinta* might have been called that in honor of the Pinto family in Palos, where the ships were readied for the voyage. But a more likely explanation: "Pinta" also means "painted lady"—sailor slang for a flirtatious woman.

• The *Niña*, smallest of the three ships, had previously been known as the *Santa Clara*. *Niña* means "little girl."

• And the *Santa María*? Many of the crew knew it by the name of *La Gallega* (*Lady from Galicia*), so-called because it was built in that region of Spain. But it had a nickname, *Marigalante*—*Dirty Mary*. The devout Columbus objected, demanding that the crew call the boat *Santa María* in honor of Jesus' mother.

MYTH #3: Queen Isabella of Spain believed so firmly in Columbus's project that she pawned her jewels to finance it.

THE TRUTH: Isabella didn't pawn anything. The queen had a special fondness for Columbus: they were both in their mid-30s, extremely religious, and enthusiastic about reforming the world. Queen Isabella would listen to Columbus for hours as he laid out his maps of the world and described his plans for carrying Christianity across the ocean. Despite that, he couldn't get her to finance his plans—her money was already being used to finance a holy war against the Islamic Moors in southern Spain.

With the defeat of Granada, the last Islamic stronghold, in January 1492, the queen was feeling generous. Columbus saw this as a good time to ask for financial backing…and he was right. Isabella was now soundly behind his vision of taking Christianity across the waters to save thousands more souls.

But she didn't need to pawn her jewels. As queen of Castile, she had plenty of resources. She used funds from her government coffers, which had been fattened by confiscating property from Jews, Muslims, and "infidels." She even figured out a way to cut expenses. Shippers in the harbor town of Palos, Spain, had been caught smuggling African goods without paying taxes. As punishment, the town was ordered to supply ships and provisions for Columbus's journey.

MYTH #4: Christopher Columbus was named… Christopher Columbus.

THE TRUTH: He was never called Columbus in his lifetime. In fact, he was known by at least five other names:

• **Cristoforo Colombo.** Most historians believe this was his given name.

• **Christovam Colom.** From when he lived in Portugal.

• **Cristóbal Colón.** He adopted this name after he moved to Spain.

- **Christophorus Colonus.** This is the name preferred by his son Fernando, who wrote a biography of his dad.

- **Xpoual de Colon.** This is what was in his official agreement with the king and queen of Spain before his first voyage across the Atlantic. After 1493, he signed his name "Xpo FERENS," using only his first name, in the fashion of royalty. Later he began to sign his name like this:

.s.

.S. A .S.

X M Y

: Xpo FERENS/

(Nobody in the past 500 years has been able to explain what this signature means.)

*   *   *

PRESIDENTIAL PETS

When Theodore Roosevelt became president in 1901, the White House literally became a zoo. Roosevelt had six children, and they loved pets. Soon the executive mansion was filled with dogs, cats, squirrels, raccoons, rabbits, guinea pigs, a badger, a black bear, a rat, a parrot and a green garter snake named Emily Spinach.

When Archie Roosevelt got the measles and had to stay in his second-floor bedroom, his brothers decided to cheer him up with a visit from his pony, Algonquin. How did the pony get up to the second floor? Same as everyone else: in the elevator.

GETTIN' JIGGY

Everything has a history—even jigsaw puzzles. They started as a toy for rich kids…became a hobby for wealthy adults…and then, when mass production made it possible, became a pastime for the rest of us.

THE FIRST JIGSAW PUZZLE

Jigsaw puzzles were one of Western Europe's first educational toys. In 1762 a London mapmaker and printer named John Spilsbury glued a few of his maps onto thin wood panels. Then, using a small handsaw, he cut them up along the borders of each country. He called them "dissected maps" and sold them to well-to-do parents "for the edification of the young."

His timing was perfect—the first children's books had been published only a year earlier, and there was a lot of interest in finding new ways to teach kids. By 1800, twenty different London publishers were cranking out puzzles. Most featured historical subjects or biblical stories. (Religious puzzles were especially popular on Sundays because a lot of kids weren't allowed to "play" on the Sabbath.)

REAL JIGSAW PUZZLES

Puzzles were made one at a time, gluing expensive prints to fine woods. Each piece was cut out with a handsaw, and each puzzle had no more than 50 pieces. Only the border pieces interlocked; anything more complicated would have cost too much money—even for the wealthy. Early puzzles cost the equivalent of a week's wages for a common laborer.

Then, in 1876, a power saw, known as the "jigsaw," was invented. It was inexpensive (some foot-powered models sold for as little as $3) and was capable of making extremely intricate cuts. It immediately revolutionized furniture design, and by the 1890s had had an impact on puzzles, too. Using a jigsaw, craftsmen made completely interlocking puzzles with smaller pieces...which could challenge kids *and* adults.

PUZZLEMANIA

The new puzzles were a big hit. Their popularity kept growing in Europe and in 1908, a jigsaw puzzle craze swept America. No one was left out: if you couldn't afford to buy puzzles, there were puzzle lending libraries and even puzzle rental companies. Sales were so strong that Parker Brothers gave up manufacturing games for a year to focus exclusively on puzzles. (It was also during the 1908 craze that they came up with the idea of cutting the pieces into shapes that people could recognize—stars, ducks, dogs, flowers, snowflakes, etc.)

THE GOLDEN AGE OF PUZZLES

When the craze died down, jigsaw puzzles had become a part of American life. By 1930 they were no longer made of wood—they were cardboard. And they weren't cut with a jigsaw—they were cut by big single press machines (but they were still called jigsaw puzzles).

And the new puzzles were cheap. It was possible to buy a beautiful puzzle for as little as 10¢.

Then came the Great Depression. The stock market crashed, companies went out of business, and a lot of people lost their jobs. People didn't have a lot of money to spend on entertainment, so these inexpensive puzzles became popular again. The result: Americans went on another puzzle-buying binge, purchasing up to six million puzzles a week! In less than one year, manufacturers sold more than $100 million worth of jigsaw puzzles (in 1930s money!).

STAND-UP GUY

Puzzles remained more or less unchanged after the 1930s...until 1989. That year, a Canadian named Paul Gallant decided to start a toy company. But he wasn't sure what kind of toys he wanted to make. He thought about puzzles and wondered why no one had ever made a 3D puzzle. He experimented with ordinary cardboard puzzle pieces, but they fell over when he tried to stand them up. So he made some out of polyethylene foam and found that the pieces were sturdy enough to build miniature walls.

In 1991 Gallant made a 3D puzzle resembling a Victorian mansion and took it to the FAO Schwarz toy store in Manhattan, where he showed it to one of the store's buyers. "I took the puzzle and I threw it in the air," Gallant says. It didn't break. "Then I separated the pieces and showed him this

---

Zebra stripes are as unique as human fingerprints. No two zebras are alike.

was really a puzzle. And he said, 'Wow, where did you get that?'" FAO Schwarz bought 74 puzzles that afternoon; Gallant's company now sells more than $100 million worth of 3D puzzles—shaped like skyscrapers, castles, the Eiffel Tower, the Titanic, and even Star Wars spaceships—every year, making it another of the biggest puzzle fads in history.

PUZZLING INNOVATIONS

Here are some unusual puzzle products you might find on your next trip to the toy store:

• **Mono-colored puzzles.** No pretty pictures, just hundreds of puzzle pieces, all painted the same color with no clue as to where they belong in the puzzle.

• **Multiple-border puzzles.** Pieces with straight edges that appear to be border pieces, but are actually inner pieces.

• **Impossibles.** 750-piece borderless puzzles. No taking the easy way out by connecting outer edges first, because edge pieces look like inner pieces. To make it even harder: five extra pieces that don't fit anywhere.

• **Triazzles.** All of the pieces are triangle-shaped with similar designs, but with only one correct solution.

• **The world's most difficult jigsaw puzzles.** Double-sided puzzles with 529 pieces. The same artwork is on the other side, rotated slightly to make it more difficult.

Ha Ha! Q: What do you get when you eat beans while you're chopping onions? A: Tear gas.

The
Back Side

You're not done yet:

Here are the answers
to the quizzes found on pages
27, 99, 149, 161, and 210...

...and info about how to be a part
of the Bathroom Readers' Institute.

ANSWERS

CELEBRITY QUIZ
(Answers from page 99.)

1. c) Natalie Portman moved from Jerusalem to Maryland when she was three. In addition to English, she can speak fluent Hebrew, French, and Japanese.

2. a) Tom Cruise listens to his lines on an audiotape because he has dyslexia, so sometimes it's hard for him to read.

3. c) One of his high school teachers thought Will Smith acted up "just like a prince," and the name stuck.

4. c) Tommy Lee Jones roomed with Al Gore, who he considers "like a brother," at Harvard University.

5. b) Vince McMahon recruited Bollea to the WWF in 1979 and named him the Incredible Hulk Hogan, a reference to the then-popular TV show *The Incredible Hulk*.

6. a) During the filming of the popular kids' TV show *Romper Room*, Leo was kicked off the set for being a brat. "I was the nuttiest little kid," he said later. "I'd smack the camera and jump around. They couldn't control me."

7. a) Sandra Bullock's mother is German opera singer Helga Meyer. As a child, Sandra would often tour with her mother's productions and even sing in the children's choir.

If you want a quiet dog, get a *Basenji*. It's the only breed that doesn't bark.

8. b) *Keanu* means "cool breeze over the mountains" in Hawaiian. But he wasn't born in Hawaii; he was born in Beirut, Lebanon, in 1964.

9. c) Haley Joel loves lizards. He owns two leopard geckos as pets and likes to catch wild lizards and release them in his backyard.

10. c) Sarah Michelle Gellar has taken Tae Kwon Do lessons for more than five years. She also spent three years as a competitive figure skater before becoming a full-time vampire slayer.

11. a) Jean-Claude took karate lessons as a child in Belgium, but as a teenager he turned to body-building...and ballet.

12. b) Even though he had already acted in movies and television, Harrison was working as a set builder in 1976 when he was asked to read for the part of Han Solo for *Star Wars*, the role that made him famous.

13. c) Because 21-year-old Drew felt he needed more self-discipline, he joined the Marine Corps in 1980. He liked the buzz cut they gave him so much that he's kept it ever since.

14. b) As a child, Maguire loved to cook, but his mother wanted him to act instead, so she offered him $100 to take drama in high school instead of home economics. He took the cash, took the drama class, and the rest is history.

Q: What's the most widely spoken language on Earth?

UNCLE JOHN'S
BRAIN TICKLERS
(Answers from page 27.)

1. Square Deal.

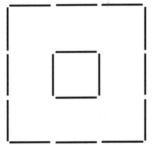

2. Going in Circles. 20. The number in the center of each circle is the sum of the three numbers on its outer edge.

UNCLE JOHN'S
TRI-CKY TRI-CKS
(Answers from page 149.)

1. You Tri My Patience.

a)

b)

2. Tri, Tri Again.

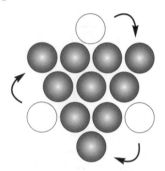

UNCLE JOHN:
PUZZLE DETECTIVE
(Answers from page 161.)

Sitting Pretty. Your lap, of course. Uncle John thought it was obvious because they were standing in front the seated statue of Lincoln. However, there was a dog standing a few feet from Uncle John—a talking dog—and he had another opinion.

"Excuse me, sir," said the dog, whose name turned out to be Elbow Room. "If I may offer an opinion, there is another solution to your puzzle."

"Do tell," said Uncle John, trying to hide his surprise.

"Your best friend may also sit next to you, a location you will never be able to inhabit."

"Amazing," said J. Porter Newman, who was beside himself with joy.

"Flying Flushes! He's right," conceded Uncle John as he walked away, followed by his trusted assistant, Newman, and his new friend...Elbow Room.

Handy Man. There were six people at the meeting. Each person shook hands five times—that makes for 15 handshakes, not 30, since each shake was shared by two people.

UNCLE JOHN'S GENIUS QUIZ
(Answers from page 210.)

1. It's A-maze-ing.

Start here

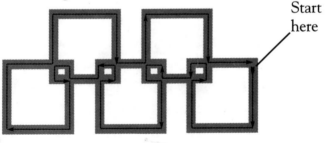

2. Row! Row! Row! Just take the first or last coin from the horizontal row and place it on top of the coin in the middle.

The five smartest primates, after humans: chimpanzees, gorillas, orangutans, baboons, gibbons.

LET YOUR VOICE BE HEARD!

Visit us at

www.bathroomreader.com

Just log on, click on our Kids' page, and tell us how good we are. We'd love to hear from you.

And while you're surfing our site, you can read articles from other *Bathroom Readers* in our "Throne Room." You can take our online polls, too. You can even join up to be a member of the BRI. (Mrs. Uncle John says: *"Make sure it's okay with your parents."*)

And speaking of parents—and teachers—we want to know what *you* think, as well. The website is the best way to contact us, but there are other ways:

BRI
P.O. Box 1117
Ashland, OR 97520

phone: (541) 488-4642
fax: (541) 482-6159

YOUR TURN!

Here's your big chance to let us know what you want in the next edition of Uncle John's Bathroom Reader for Kids Only. *Write it down here, cut it out, and send it to us.*

_____

_____

_____

_____

_____

_____

_____

_____

_____

_____

_____

_____

Need more space? Find more paper!

THE LAST PAGE

FELLOW BATHROOM READERS:
Bathroom reading should never be taken loosely—we must sit firmly for what we believe in, even while the rest of the world is taking pot shots at us.

Sit Down and Be Counted! Join the Bathroom Readers' Institute. It's free! Send a self-addressed, stamped envelope to: BRI, P.O. Box 1117, Ashland, Oregon 97520. Or contact us through our website at *www.bathroomreader.com*. You'll receive a free membership card, our BRI newsletter (sent out via e-mail), discounts when ordering directly through the BRI, and you'll earn a permanent spot on the BRI honor roll!

UNCLE JOHN'S NEXT *BATHROOM READER FOR KIDS ONLY* IS IN THE WORKS!

Don't fret—there's more good reading on the way.

• Is there a subject you'd like to see us research? Write to us or contact us through our website and let us know. We aim to please.

Well, we're out of space, and when you've got to go, you've got to go. Hope to hear from you soon. Meanwhile, remember:

Go with the Flow!